Be Agile Do Agile

Be Agile Do Agile

Vittal S. Anantatmula and Timothy J. Kloppenborg

BEP

BUSINESS EXPERT PRESS

Leader in applied, concise business books

Be Agile Do Agile

Copyright © Business Expert Press, LLC, 2021.

Cover design by Charlene Kronstedt

Interior design by Exeter Premedia Services Private Ltd., Chennai, India

First published in 2021 by
Business Expert Press, LLC
222 East 46th Street, New York, NY 10017
www.businessexpertpress.com

ISBN-13: 978-1-95334-994-1 (paperback)
ISBN-13: 978-1-95334-995-8 (e-book)

Business Expert Press Portfolio and Project Management Collection

Collection ISSN: 2156-8189 (print)
Collection ISSN: 2156-8200 (electronic)

First edition: 2021

10 9 8 7 6 5 4 3 2 1

This book is dedicated

Manga Anantatmula
Elizabeth Kloppenborg

for their invaluable support

Description

The global economy and free market philosophy have resulted in higher global competition and increased expectations from customers. It is obvious that new approaches are needed to satisfy demands and many of them fall under a broad umbrella called agile. To capitalize fully on the benefits of agile, one must first understand the concepts that underpin it.

In this book, we first identify many concepts that various approaches advocate for agile and group them into three areas forming a simple, robust system. Then, we describe the most useful agile methods in savage summaries regardless of the approach that promotes them, grouping them logically and showing how to use them.

We have an agnostic agile model that can be useful to anyone using any form of agile. Both concepts for being agile and techniques for doing agile are summarized in this book and there are several ways to use this book. To understand the concepts of agile, consult Chapters 3, 4, and 5. Chapters 7, 8, and 9 will help you learn and perform agile tools and techniques.

Keywords

agile; agile mindset; agile tools; agile metrics; agile manifesto; lean; scrum; XP; SAFe; disciplined agile; project; project leadership; project success; project management; leadership; servant leadership; emergent leadership; teamwork; roles

Contents

Acknowledgments

We would like to thank Frank Forte and Andy Burns who are both agile gurus and have taught us a great deal. We would also like to thank our four reviewers, Frank Forte, Kathryn Wells, Laurie Laning, and Marcie Lensges, who each offered different perspectives and useful suggestions. Finally, we would like to thank our editor Kam Jugdev who found more ideas for improvement.

CHAPTER 1

Introduction

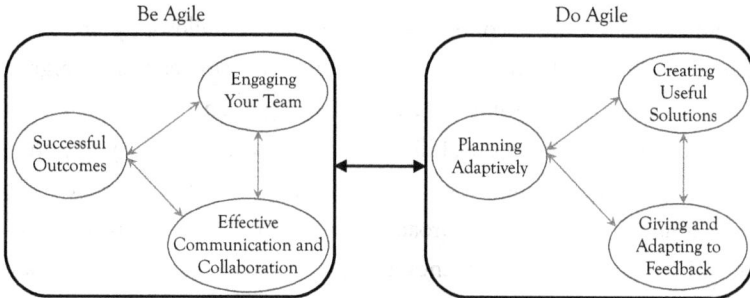

Be Agile   Do Agile

Engaging Your Team

Successful Outcomes   Planning Adaptively   Creating Useful Solutions

Effective Communication and Collaboration   Giving and Adapting to Feedback

With the onset of personal computers in 1980s and becoming popular in 1990s, an urgent need to develop and implement software projects became a norm and a requirement. However, for many software developers and those who sought software programs, it is an unknown territory plagued with many unknowns and uncertainties. Neither the company seeking those services nor the project team members who were attempting to deliver those projects knew what processes to adapt for delivering requisite outcomes. Then, what persuaded organizations and software developers to run into this fast-paced situation of developing projects?

The following issues are addressed briefly in this chapter and with more details in the book.

1. Tell why organizations have turned to agile as a method of planning and managing their projects
2. Briefly describe major differences between plan-driven (traditional) and agile project management
3. Describe why agile is sometimes a more useful approach
4. Briefly define what *be agile* and *do agile* mean

The answer is simple. Personal computers and their applications presented many opportunities to improve productivity and generated many business opportunities to offer new products and services worldwide. Computerization attracted every industry—manufacturing, production, engineering, health care, research and development, service sector—and the like, you name it! Everyone was eager to adapt this technology, and you will find an enthusiastic customer for all these projects.

Further, the global economy and free market philosophy are compelling drastic changes in global competition with corresponding higher expectations from customers. These challenges and fluid situations demand agility. Agility is the ability to move quickly and easily responding to changing customer desires. An agile approach is a necessity, not an option. Obviously, this approach is necessary to manage projects, as some of the traditional approaches, designed for stable work culture, may not work. Creative and imaginative efforts of many led to the development of new approaches. Many of these fall under a broad umbrella called agile. Many projects in the current economy face a fluid situation and uncertainty that demands agility.

With so many players—customer organizations and software development companies—involved in rapid development of new applications and services, new inventions were emerging at a rapid pace. Obviously, change was becoming a norm; requirements for many projects were changing routinely. Some projects were canceling altogether, as their intended outcomes were becoming obsolete even before the delivery, as customers were redefining project objectives to catch up with competitors and market demand. Business was moving at fast pace. Consequently, traditional project management methods were set aside, as they mismatched the demands of these new projects. These projects were often referred to as *application development by crisis*. These hazy circumstances led to thinking of agility in planning and executing projects.

Around the same time, with the advent of information technology and its applications, business and customers alike were expecting products and services faster, better, and cheaper. Further, the information technology sector facilitated this change in mindset by explosion of information sharing and expansion of the market globally. A major change was also occurring in the IT world—which is data management. Large subject databases were being implemented to manage data as a corporate asset. This meant that applications no longer had to create all their own data and manage it. Applications could now tap into high-quality data sources quickly. Therefore, the speed at which applications could be developed increased dramatically. People and organizations liked this opportunity and placed higher demands for quality products and services at an affordable rate. All these changes left no option for project managers but to consider agility in project planning and execution.

Traditional project management methods and tools were developed during the period prior to information age that was less chaotic. Project management, as a formal discipline, began in early 1950s, and proponents of the systemic approach developed traditional project management methodology. After the agile approach is developed, this traditional approach is often referred to as *waterfall methodology* and justifiably so. In this traditional or waterfall method, a project usually transitions from one phase to the next phase sequentially and usually after the previous phase is completed. For example, one must understand all the requirements that identify exclusions, inclusions, assumptions, specifications, and constraints associated with the project deliverable, and then the scope of a project is defined. Without scope definition, project plan activities cannot be initiated, and without developing a comprehensive project plan, we cannot move forward to the project execution phase. This traditional approach is systematic, logical, and makes sense when technology and engineering associated with these projects have been steady and changes are gradual. However, it is not true with information technology, which is changing by leaps and bounds.

Specifically, software development projects are faced with rapid and constant growth of technology and associated changes in customer demands. Clients often do not know what they want in a new system or product, and younger workers chafe at old command and control restrictions. At the best, a customer can explain the work process and flow (context of the project) and the desired functional outcomes expected from the project. In many cases, the software development effort takes a trial-and-error approach to identify features and use quality tests to ensure customer satisfaction. The critical challenge is to translate a need or requirement into a specification, which is not easy in this case. This is one of the main reasons why an agile approach is justified. Other reasons for employing agile methods are ambiguous and changing requirements of the project and compelling forces of global economy to deliver products and services faster, better, and cheaper.

In addition to the nature of changes to the projects and global economy, the U.S. government also permitted an iterative process of project planning and execution in 1990s. An *iterative process* is a method to plan the entire project at only a high level at the start and plan portions to be done soon in detail, updating plans as more becomes known. This was one of the main reasons why iterative project planning processes gained popularity, and one can see the number of applications. The agile (aka change-driven) methodology is a project method using iterative and continual processes and is guided by agile mindset described in the *Agile Manifesto* and elaborated by many sources. Agile found its acceptance among the project management professionals and in the corporate world.

The first agile method that became popular was scrum in 1990s. When developing new and complex products, the project team will be informed of the project objectives, and the team will have autonomy of actions to deliver these objectives. Subsequently, many other variations of the agile approach have evolved. One of the main purposes of this book is to identify concepts that various agile approaches advocate and assemble them into simple, but a comprehensive system. It is our intent to identify the most common and most useful agile mindset ideas and methods regardless of the approach, group them logically, and explain how to use them effectively.

When and Why Agile Should Be Used

One of the compelling reasons for the use of an agile method is the difficulty associated with defining requirements of a project. A *requirement* "is a condition or capability needed by a user to solve a problem or achieve an objective that satisfies a standard, a specification, or any other formally documented need" (Kloppenborg, Anantatmula and Wells 2018; p. 212). Further, a requirement should unambiguous, complete, usable, and verifiable. Requirement definition and conditions associated with it cannot easily be defined in the case of a software or similar project where the technology and customer needs are constantly evolving. This work situation compels project managers and teams to reject traditional project management and adopt agile methods.

A good example to illustrate the dynamic nature of projects is the way many organizations are responding to the COVID-19 pandemic situation and developing new online solutions for businesses that were providing services at a facility previously. These solutions differ based on the nature of the business, location of the business, and the government restrictions imposed at that location. And, these changes are dynamic and dictated by local, state, and federal governments. Many other organizations, governments, and other services are adapting their businesses to these social changes. One can imagine the changing nature of requirements and incremental improvements of solutions of projects that are aimed to provide solutions.

Plan-Driven (Traditional) Versus Agile Project Management

Plan-driven (aka predictive, traditional, or waterfall) is an approach to projects where the entire project is planned in detail early in the project, and great effort is expended to control any changes. While all of those terms are used somewhat interchangeably, for this book, we will use the term *plan-driven*, as it is easy to understand the contrast with agile. Both the plan-driven and agile projects are conceived to meet one or a combination of the following reasons:

- Market demand
- Organizational need
- Customer request
- Technological advance
- Legal requirements
- Social need (specific for a nonprofit organization)
- Crisis situation
- Replacement or update of obsolete technology or equipment

Table 1.1 Plan-driven versus agile philosophy

Plan-driven (traditional)	Change-driven (agile)
• Management as planning • Dispatching model for executing • Thermostat model for control	• Management as organizing for planning • Action perspective for execution • Scientific experimentation for control

While the reasons for initiating a project may find commonality, management philosophy of the plan-driven method and agile method differs (Table 1.1).

Plan-driven project management presents a transformation view of production. Three theories of management are considered for plan-driven project management (Koskela and Howell 2002), and they are: management as planning, dispatching model for execution, and thermostat model for control. Project execution is based on a comprehensive project plan, which is finalized to ensure that project execution is accomplished strictly based on that plan. The plan also provides measures for progress and completion, and they are monitored constantly. This approach is suitable when we have a fairly good understanding of the project scope, and deliverables are specified accurately. In other words, uncertainties and unknowns associated with the project are few, and dealing with changes may not be challenging or disruptive. In general, the project-executing organization and the project team are qualified with adequate experience and expertise to complete the project successfully. The planned approach has its premise on minimizing uncertainties and unknowns. Consequently, the plan-driven project management approach may not deal with complexity and changes associated with uncertainty and unknowns.

When projects are afflicted with a lack of full understanding of the outcomes, fast-paced technological changes, and unclear needs of the client, a plan-driven project management approach may prove to be inadequate. The client may reveal functional outcomes incrementally as the project makes progress, and the results are assessed. In other words, these projects are associated with uncertainties and change. And, to deal with them, a project team's immediate focus is on flow and value generation. The agile or change-driven approach is better suited for these projects with a focus on:

- Management as organizing for planning
- Action perspective for execution
- Scientific experimentation model for control

Management as organizing means the emphasis is on developing the team structure and encouraging the team to perform needed planning, only as much as is needed to execute each portion of work. Progress is controlled by gaining feedback early and often and discussion of what worked, what did not work, and why. This approach of management creating the conditions whereby a team can plan, perform, and use results and judgment to control progress differs starkly from plan-driven approach of management as planning and thermostat model for control.

In the plan-driven project method, requirements are defined in the beginning of the project (upfront planning), and then it will be signed off for the project manager to freeze before the design and implementation phase is started sequentially. The project manager uses a strict command and control style using formal communication and a mechanistic structure to ensure that the work is completed as planned. However, in an agile project, iterative planning is adapted, and only high-level objectives are defined at the beginning of the project. Then, a detailed requirement prioritization is done iteratively in later stages of the project. Leaders (who probably do not have the title project manager) use collaboration with team members, communicating informally to organically and flexibly develop solutions that will help their clients achieve desired outcomes (Table 1.2).

The fundamental difference between the two approaches is that instead of freezing specifications early and developing a fixed plan, the agile approach adapts flexibility to modify and alter project plans to address critical business needs. An agile method is employed when:

- The project scope is unclear or poorly defined
- Required task times are unknown or unknowable
- Tasks and task dependencies are unknown
- The availability of resources is unknown or continuously changing

A decision to adapt agile under these circumstances is justified, as it offers greater adaptability to frequently changing scope, uses iterative or phased planning, continuous integration, promotes collaboration, and improves customer satisfaction.

Table 1.2 Plan-driven versus agile development

	Traditional development	**Agile development**
Assumption	Systems are fully specifiable, predictable, and are built through meticulous and extensive planning	High-quality adaptive software is developed by small teams using the principles of continuous design improvement and testing based on rapid feedback and change
Management style	Command and control	Leadership and collaboration
Knowledge	Explicit	Tacit
Communication	Formal	Informal
Model	Lifecycle	Evolutionary delivery
Structure	Mechanistic	Organic
Quality control	Planning and strict control	Continuous control of requirements, design, and solutions

Source: Dybå and Dingsøyr, 2008.

What Is the Plan-Driven Method?

It is well known that projects are constrained by scope, time, and cost. Quality, for the most part, is integral to scope. As it is a nonroutine endeavor, everything about a project is not known to us; we often term them as unknowns and uncertainties. Also, the client may change requirements based on new ideas or if an original and documented requirement is not feasible, not required, or it becomes obsolete during the project implementation stage. With the change in requirements, the project scope changes, which also leads to changes in cost and schedule. As everything about a project is not known, we make certain assumptions, and if these assumptions go wrong, then also the project scope, cost, and time will change. For example, we may assume that appropriate resources (quantity and quality) are available as and when required during the project execution. Some projects tend to be complex, that is, we know what we prefer as an outcome of the project, but we do not know how to accomplish it. Obviously, an inherent characteristic of a project is risk. Project risks are due to:

- Inaccurate or unrealistic assumptions
- Lack of complete understanding of the project scope
- Uncertainties

- Unknowns
- Changes to project scope, cost, and schedule due to unanticipated constraints
- Complexity associated with the project
- Inaccurate estimations of cost, schedule, and risk

In a plan-driven or traditional approach, we may attempt to address these issues to the extent possible while developing the project plan, but there is no such thing as a perfect project plan. If there is something constant about projects, it is the change.

Another important aspect is the distinction between a project and process. A process consists of a series of actions designed to bring about a result, be it a product or service. A process uses a lock-step approach, and it is repeated. However, a project is complex, nonroutine, and one-time effort. Once project goals are accomplished, the project is terminated. The key differences between processes and projects are processes are repetitive and ongoing and produce the same result, whereas projects are time-bound and unique. However, project management employs several inter-dependent processes for its completion. These processes fall into two categories: project management processes and project deliverable (product or service) processes. Project management from initiation to project closeout is not always sequential (Figure 1.1).

As shown Figure 1.1, project phases are not always sequential due to risks, changes, and quality control, which forces a project management team to go back to the drawing board. From project initiation to project closeout phase, managing a project sometimes necessitates us to revisit the previous project phase. Therefore, we argue that it is not accurate to label the plan-driven or traditional project management as *waterfall* method.

Managing projects is challenging, as projects often do not have precedence or prior knowledge and deal with revolutionary improvements. Added to this, a project manager's mission is to manage conflicting and interdependent goals of delivering the product or service:

- At the client's specifications or better
- On the promised delivery date or sooner
- With the approved budget or under

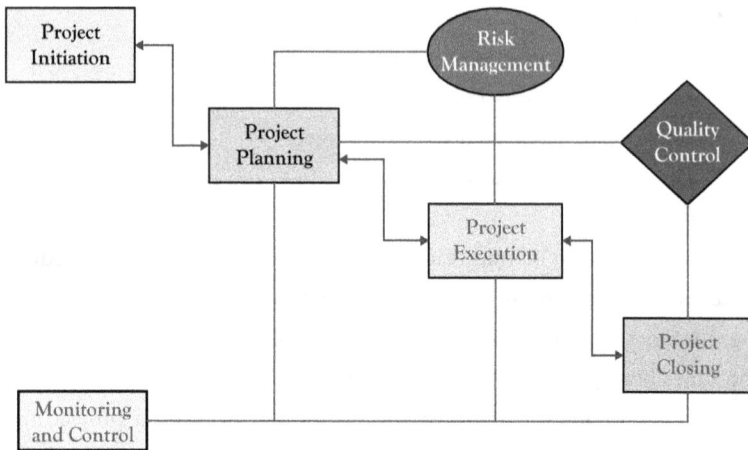

Figure 1.1 Project management process

With the global economy and free market philosophy, key stake-holders expect project teams to deliver project outcomes that are better than originally planned, complete the project earlier than the planned completion date, and at a lower cost than the planned.

Plan-driven project management offers many benefits such as:

- Early identification of project risks
- Informed and accurate schedules
- Early warning when milestones cannot be met
- Objective baseline for tradeoff analysis
- Clear functional responsibilities
- Methodically measured accomplishment reports
- Improved planning capability for future projects

However, projects may fail for many reasons such as:

- When requirements are incomplete
- When a user is not involved in planning and execution
- Nonavailability of resources
- Unrealistic expectations
- Lack of executive support
- Frequent changes to specifications

- Lack of proper planning
- Product or service is no longer needed

How Agile Is Sometimes Better Than Plan-Driven?

Plan-driven project management has its focus on the triple constraints of time, cost, and scope and its process-oriented approach. On the other hand, agile project management has its focus on business value and solutions to situations. It is an outcome-oriented approach. Plan-driven projects use distributed work teams and specialists, whereas agile project teams are ideally colocated or at least virtually colocated. They are composed of generalized specialists who are capable of doing a wider variety of tasks to manage rapid changes and increments, and it demands greater commitment from the team members. Although external forces such as the global economy, free market philosophy, and challenging situations like COVID-19 make pure colocated difficult or impossible, the benefits of working closely together are still highly desired and sought.

The plan-driven approach requires us to develop a comprehensive project plan before project execution. However, this is not feasible when projects deal with technologies that are not completely developed or unfamiliar. In those cases, an agile method would be a better option than the traditional approach of managing projects. However, we must note that new technology is one ingredient of complexity that agile aims to address. The compelling reason for the decision is our inability to define project requirements. In such projects, we tend to develop the project incrementally and in phases, allowing the plan to unfold over the time by prioritizing functions that are more beneficial to the client and delivering them. It would give the project team flexibility in focusing on important functional outcomes first instead of dealing with greater complexity. It would also benefit the client as budget is prioritized to maximize benefits. Also, the cost of rework is minimized. All these advantages would be absent if we adapt traditional approach for such technology-driven projects. Further, the project cost implications could be catastrophic if the entire project is completely planned and resources are allocated for a project where neither the client nor the project team is clear about project outcomes.

First Understand and Be Agile, Then Do Agile

Performing some of the agile methods without understanding the needed agile mindset ay produce some results, but may even result in some confusion and backlash. Therefore, we strongly believe it is important to understand, at least a little bit, or the agile mindset to start.

Be Agile

For successful adaption of an agile method, it is critical to develop an agile mindset. For those organizations that have been practicing plan-driven project management methods, it would be a paradigm shift in planning and executing projects. To sustain and improve project performance, this change in mindset must use a top-down approach. The organization, project managers, and project team members must understand and internalize agile project method principles. They include values associated with various agile methods, such as *scrum* pillars and values, and XP core values and practices. In a nutshell, the agile method advocates the following:

- Use a simple approach
- Embrace change
- Change incrementally
- Maximize value to the client
- Provide rapid feedback to all stakeholders
- Practice transparency to build trust
- Improve quality of people, processes, and products

The majority of the benefits that we accrue comes from understanding agile as the implementation strategy, and agile methods are dependent on the characteristics of the project. In other words, the agile strategy would depend on the type of project at hand.

Part of *understanding agile* is how *Agile Manifesto* principles are transformed into various practical streams of agile such as *scrum*, XP, *lean*, Scaled Agile Framework (SAFe), and disciplined agile. Only after a comprehensive understanding of these agile streams and associated benefits are understood, one can select an appropriate agile method for the project. An understanding is not enough; belief and inclusion of agile principles—by project team members, project managers, senior management, internal and external stakeholders, and the organization itself—are essential prerequisites to *doing agile*.

Do Agile

To begin with, *doing agile* requires a clear understanding of the type of project at hand. In general, projects can be divided into four categories (Figure 1.2).

1. Goal is clear—solution is clear
2. Goal clear—solution is unclear
3. Goal is unclear—solution is unclear
4. Goal is unclear—solution is clear

The fourth option is not possible because when the goal is not clear, how can we have clarity about the solution? Even if you say that a solution is clear, which goal is it trying to achieve? It is possible to consider an agile approach to manage projects of the first three categories. However, the fourth category does not seem feasible. The agile strategy would also

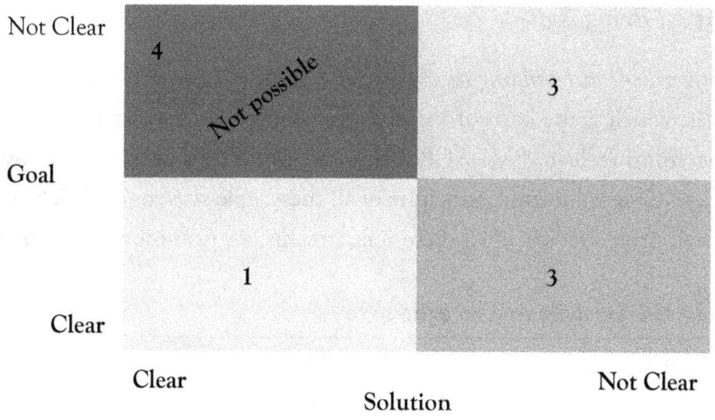

Figure 1.2 Agile strategy

Source: Wysocki 2006.

depend on project priority, delivery date, level of quality, and desired visibility of the project. Further, agile strategy is also influenced by the project team and the client. A comprehensive understanding of these issues and complete preparedness for all these strategies is critical before selecting the appropriate agile stream and associated values. The purpose of this book is to provide a detailed account of both the aspects—understanding agile, then doing agile—to manage agile projects effectively and successfully.

How the Rest of the Book Is Organized

This book has two parts. Part A of the book presents the concepts and practices associated with understanding agile, and Part B of the book consists of the tools, techniques, and metrics of doing agile, as shown in Table 1.3.

Part A presents comprehensive information to understand agile, and it consists of four chapters, namely: Understanding the Agile Mindset; Successful Outcomes; Leadership and Teamwork, including Roles and Responsibilities; and Communication and Collaboration. Part B focus is on doing agile or practices associated with managing agile practices. This part consists of four chapters, namely, Summary of Doing Agile Tools, Techniques, and Metrics; Planning Adaptively; Creating Useful Solutions; and Giving and Adapting to Feedback.

Part A: Being Agile

Chapter 2: Understanding the Agile Mindset presents *Agile Manifesto* principles, which is the basis of various agile streams such as scrum, extreme programming, lean, PMI-ACP, SAFe, and disciplined agile use as a foundation. Core values and principles of all these agile streams are briefly discussed. After a review of all these agile streams, we propose an agile model

Table 1.3 Be agile and do agile here

• **Be Agile**	• **Do Agile**
• Successful Outcomes	• Planning Adaptively
• Engaging Your Team	• Creating Useful Solutions
• Communication and Collaboration	• Giving and Adapting to Feedback

for a better understanding of the key factors and associated elements with each key factor to manage agile projects effectively and efficiently.

Chapter 3: Successful Outcomes discusses the vision and value based upon stakeholders' needs along with concepts of simplicity, excellence, and improvement. We start with considering the importance of vision at the project, project team, and organization levels. The vision must be aligned with an organization's objectives and goals. Integral to the vision is understanding stakeholders and their needs and delivering value to all the stakeholders. Simplicity is focused on work that is absolutely necessary to avoid unnecessary work and rework. Then, focus on doing it with excellence provides value to all the key stakeholders. Excellence work results in high-quality deliverables that enable users to achieve their goals. The aim is to improve products, processes, and people continuously.

Chapter 4: Leadership and Teamwork takes an approach that is different from the traditional approach of top-down leadership of command and control. In this chapter, we present concepts such as servant leadership, emergent leadership, self-managed teams, respect for all team members, selection of motivated people, creating avenues for motivation, and participative decision making. Our discussion in this chapter also includes roles and responsibilities of the team leader, team members, product owner, and technical leader.

Chapter 5: Communication and Collaboration. In a project situation of uncertainties, and absence of complete understanding of desired outcomes of the project, effective communication is critical. Face-to-face meetings, transparency, and frequent interactions with the client to receive timely feedback are critical constituents of effective communication. Team members need to collaborate effectively with each other and with various stakeholders.

Part B: Doing Agile

6. Performing Agile Methods. The *Agile Manifesto* was all about the mindset of agile, so we draw no tools or metrics from it. However, we draw upon the tools and metrics from each of the approaches mentioned so far: scrum, XP, lean or Kanban, PMI-ACP, SAFe, and disciplined agile. As with the mindset ideas, we attribute techniques to the agile approach that we feel makes the largest contribution to each. Many of the techniques are used by more than one approach.

7. Planning Adaptively. This chapter starts with using an agile lifecycle whether that cycle is based upon iterations, continuous flow, or hybrid. Second, we discuss governance of agile projects—both from the standpoint of the team monitoring their own performance and from that of others in the organization who need reassurance that the team is progressing well. We touch on systems thinking. Then, we include initial planning of envisioning the entire project, understanding user stories, prioritizing requirements and work, and guiding initial improvement efforts. Finally, we introduce the concept of ongoing planning that is expanded in the following chapter.

8. Creating Useful Solutions. This chapter starts with the tools and metrics for product planning generally and those specific to increment-based agile and lean-based agile. It includes tools for continual planning, building solutions, monitoring and controlling progress, testing, and quality.

9. Giving and Adapting to Feedback. This chapter starts with the tools for visual communication. The second section includes ideas for conducting effective sprint meetings of the following four types: planning, standup, demo, and retrospective. The third major section of this chapter is testing, followed by working through problems. We conclude the chapter by discussing improvements.

Summary

Agile is a fundamentally different approach to managing projects. When clients do not know upfront what they want in terms of deliverables and are willing to learn with the development team as progress is made, agile may be appropriate. Team members take a more active role in planning and managing their own work, and the role of project manager may be split between the team, a product owner, and a facilitator known as a scrum master. Early results lead to informed decisions as the details of deliverables emerge.

The goal is not to merely deliver according to specification, on time, and on budget. Rather, the primary goal is to help the client become successful using the results of the project. This is an important distinction. Often, using traditional project management methods on large complex projects, such as implementing an enterprise resource planning (ERP) system with new work processes, an additional project phase would have to be added. This additional project phase will focus on delivering the promised business benefits by learning how to leverage the new system capabilities and new work processes.

Questions

1. Tell why organizations have turned to agile as a method of planning and managing their projects.
2. Briefly describe major differences between plan-driven (traditional) and agile project management.
3. Describe why agile is sometimes a more useful approach.
4. Briefly define what *be agile* and *do agile* mean.

PART I

Being Agile

CHAPTER 2

Understanding the Agile Mindset

Be Agile   Do Agile

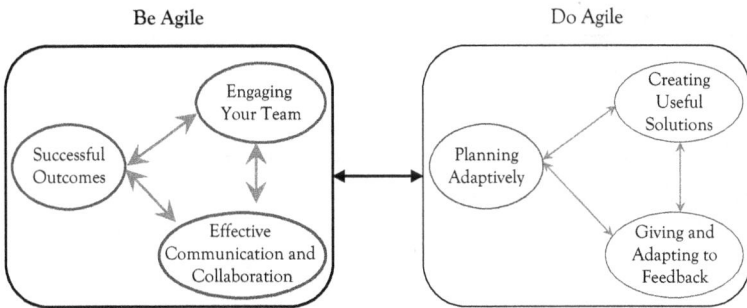

This chapter focuses on how to be agile, rather than do agile. In other words, what shifts in understanding do people need to have to fully embrace and capitalize upon the potential benefits of agile? These shifts in understanding have been described as values, principles, and pillars, and we briefly introduce each as they are described in the Agile Manifesto. We discuss mindset ideas from scrum, extreme programming (XP), lean, and PMI-ACP Exam Outline for understanding how to apply agile directly on a project. We then discuss ideas from Scaled Agile Framework and Disciplined Agile to see how an organization needs to change to be agile.

The following issues are addressed briefly in this chapter and with more details in the book.

1. Describe the importance of understanding what agile and why it is appropriate for certain projects
2. Briefly describe major advantages of agile method
3. Describe principles of agile method and agile manifesto
4. Present various agile methods and their key ideas

Table 2.1 Key contributions from each agile approach

Agile approach	Key contributions
Manifesto	Value individuals, working product, collaboration, and response to change
Scrum	Planning and managing
XP	Technical and feedback
Lean	Maintain flow, limit waste
Project Management Institute (PMI)	Vision and leadership
Scaled Agile Framework (SAFe)	Scaling and quality
Disciplined Agile	Lifecycles and measuring outcomes

Further, we list key contributions of each approach in Table 2.1 and describe them in the remainder of this chapter.

Often more than one framework stresses the same concept, and we only describe each concept as advocated by the agile approach that we feel places more emphasis on it and describes it better. Some of the concepts we present in this chapter are hard to define without referring to a technique that is introduced in Chapter 6. When we feel a technique needs to be introduced in this chapter, we put it with a very brief description in a textbox. Many of the concepts introduced by various agile approaches originated in software development. While some of the language still appears oriented specifically to information technology projects, when possible, we try to create descriptions that apply to a wider variety of projects. We end the chapter with a summary of the understanding of key agile concepts people need in one framework.

Manifesto Values and Principles

The Agile Manifesto was written and signed in 2001 by leading successful software design project managers who were frustrated with traditional project management. They had been experimenting with alternative approaches for some time and had strong ideas of how traditional project management failed on many information technology (IT) projects. The primary reason is that traditional project management, which they refer to as waterfall, tells managers to create a full plan before executing the project work and managing any proposed changes very aggressively. This traditional approach works well for many industrial projects where the deliverables being built can be understood in detail at the outset. However, for many knowledge projects (such as creating new concepts, research, and software) where the client does not know what they want in detail and/or conditions are changing rapidly, the old methods stifle rather than enhance projects. For these knowledge projects, use of the agile approach is justified. The Agile Manifesto is composed of four values and 12 principles.

Four Manifesto Principles

The four Agile Manifesto principles form the heart of the agile mindset. Each of the principles includes two thoughts, as we show in Table 2.2. The one on the left is valued more highly than the one on the right, but the one on the right is still important.

1. Value individuals more than processes.
The first value states that individuals are valued more than processes. This acknowledges most workers are thinking, caring, committed people who want to do good work, and are flexible when figuring out specifics of how to accomplish certain things. Good work processes are also needed, but inflexible processes often stifle innovation and limit potential results. Rigid processes also frustrate thinking individuals.

2. Value working software more than documentation.
The second value states working software is more important than early, comprehensive documentation. The entire reason a project is undertaken is to create something with value. Documentation, while useful and

Table 2.2 Agile Manifesto principles

Manifesto adherents value this column	More than this column
Individuals and their development and ideas	Work processes
Working product delivered early and often	Detailed documentation created early
Effective customer collaboration	Tense negotiations
Response to change even late in a project	Strict following of a detailed plan

necessary sometimes, does not need to come first. In fact, with changes that may be enacted, extensive documentation early may force significant rework later. It is better to start with minimal documentation and add to it as decisions are solidified.

3. Value customer collaboration more than negotiation.

Collaboration up and down the supply chain with suppliers and customers is helpful in discovering the best ways to do work and to resolve problems. Hard-nosed negotiation is an example of transaction mentality where one is looking for the very best deal at the present without worrying about consequences. This leads to very expensive changes and inflexible agreements. Negotiation is also needed, but principled negotiation with an eye toward effective partnerships is the way to go.

4. Value response to change over following a plan.

In many dynamic industries, change happens quickly. Responding to those changes is often more helpful than adhering to a plan. Traditional project management recognizes that if you have a rigid plan, late change in a project is often quite expensive and disruptive. Agile projects actually are planned carefully. The difference between an agile (or change-driven) approach and a traditional (or planned-driven) approach is that in agile projects, planning occurs bit by bit as more is understood. Therefore, the resulting plans tend to be much better informed and useful. Those plans may change at any time.

Twelve Manifesto Principles

The 12 Agile Manifesto principles elaborate upon the four values. These principles are still much more mindset or *being agile* than they are prescriptions for techniques or *doing Agile*. As such, we cover all of them here.

1. Customer satisfaction is given the highest priority.

The very reason for conducting a project is that someone or some group(s) need the results. Therefore, one of the most important considerations for any decision always needs to be how will this impact the people who are using the outputs of this project. If there are later customers in the supply chain, the question is broader—how will this impact anyone else who needs to work on this *and* how will it impact those people who use the ultimate results of this project?

One further aspect of giving customer satisfaction the highest priority is this alters how people view the old iron triangle. That approach says cost, schedule, and scope can be traded off against each other. One needs to be most important and the others need to be flexible. When customer satisfaction is highest, anything else may need to be traded off to enhance customer satisfaction.

2. Unlike traditional approach, changes in requirements are appreciated even during the project executing phase, with a view to exploit competitive advantage for the customer.

Agile values the opportunity to make changes whenever they are in the customer's best interest. Often, a change, even late in a project, can give the customer greater value. Remembering customer satisfaction is key (see preceding point), agile teams continually look for how to improve a project when it may help a customer.

3. Present working software to the client frequently during the project execution phase.

This principle expands upon the value of working software being important. If working software (function or working product or service of whatever type is being created on the project) is important, then it is useful to get usable portions of it into the client hands quickly and often. This has one advantage of obtaining rapid feedback, so the project team can more quickly understand exactly what the users want. Plans can then be firmed up. It is also quite handy because as the client is more excited about the early project results, they will champion the project, making many aspects easier.

4. People representing business and development team must work together constantly.

One lament many traditional project managers have is that it is difficult to meet frequently enough with decision makers. If one must wait for a decision to be made, it will slow down the project. Moreover, the workers then turn their sights to other work, and the resulting disruption often impacts quality. Having those folks who understand thoroughly the business reasons for a project, available both to make decisions and also to provide frequent input, will help in making better and more rapid decisions. The project is completed sooner and better, and everyone involved is more satisfied.

5. Project team comprised of motivated people must be engaged in the project; support and trust must be extended to the project team.

This principle gets to the heart of leadership instead of management. Leaders in agile projects must understand that, to enable teams to be truly motivated, one must start with good people with a belief that they are good. One needs to create a culture of trust. Trust may take a long time to build, but can be destroyed quickly. Therefore, it is vital, especially in the heat of difficult situations, to always support and show trust for the team members.

6. Face-to-face communication must be employed, which is considered effective and efficient. In other words, it is preferable to have a colocated project team.

As projects are conducted for and with many people, effective communication is essential. The hottest (most effective) communications occur face to face where people can see gestures and body language and hear nuances of voice. Majority of communication is nonverbal. Also, as many little things need to be coordinated on most projects, having people together is ideal. However, that is often impractical, so all kinds of systems are sometimes used to create a virtual meeting space. The primary idea behind this principle is to have as much communication as possible through the most effective channels and as little as possible through colder channels such as e-mail.

7. Project progress is the progress made in developing working software.

Getting working product into the hands of a customer or at least the representative of customers allows them to try it out. They can determine what works well and suggest ways to improve it. The sooner this happens, the less rework will need to occur and the more satisfied the customers will be. Therefore, the real test of how a project is proceeding is how much usable product and when it can be delivered to customers.

8. Agile process is meant to create sustainable development, which demands sponsors, developers, and users work at the same pace for a long period.

Most project customers want the results of their projects as quickly as possible so that they can begin to use them. Beyond that, many projects are time-sensitive, as there is a window of opportunity. Because of the urge to deliver project results quickly, there is often pressure on project teams to work extra-long hours. This might be feasible for very short periods of time, but should be minimized. Agile management recognizes that projects are completed by people, and if we can sustain those people through reasonable schedules, they will continue to be productive, energetic, careful, and innovative in the long run.

9. Uninterrupted attention to technical excellence and good design boosts agility.

By creating a good product in the first place, better product will get into the hands of customers. One good way to create good deliverables is to insist on using good methods and standards and carefully check as one goes along. Having workers check their own work and share openly with their colleagues for further checks helps to discover problems early and deliver better quality products.

10. Simplicity—the art of maximizing the amount of work not done—is essential.

The systems developed on many projects include features and functions that are seldom used. If one can only deliver the portions of deliverables that will be used extensively, then quicker, less expensive, and better-quality products are created. This truly enables agile teams to deliver better, faster, and cheaper—the holy grail of excelling in all aspects of traditional tradeoffs.

11. Self-managed teams help develop the best architectures, requirements, and designs.

When team members decide among themselves who will do what and how will the team approach work, better ideas emerge. This is the essence of recognizing the workers who perform our projects are thinking, feeling, proud people. They want to do their best work, and by encouraging them to use their whole self, they will create the best deliverables that they feel pride in developing and users will be happy using.

12. If not daily, the team routinely considers how to improve effectiveness and amends its behavior accordingly.

We can all learn lessons, big and small, from the work we do. The more frequently individuals and teams assess what has worked well and what can be improved, the quicker they will improve. Also, if this assessment is frequent, many little things that might be forgotten in time will be addressed, and many little improvements add up.

Scrum Pillars and Values

In the next several sections of this chapter, we cover a few of the additional thoughts expressed by adherents of the major streams of agile that expand upon the Agile Manifesto values and principles. The major agile systems, such as scrum and XP, generally list ideas that expand upon the original Agile Manifesto and include some ideas that we classify as being agile—that is, understanding and believing agile behaviors and some ideas that we classify as doing agile—the mechanics of agile practices. Some of the ideas may have a bit of being and doing, and we classify them where we think they fit best. Further, several approaches to agile expand upon the Manifesto in similar ways, and we choose the method that we believe most clearly articulates the idea for inclusion in our lists. A few ideas such as respect have different aspects promoted by different approaches, and we include each. Regardless of where an idea originates, we end this chapter by tying all of the ideas into one coherent whole.

We start with the most commonly practiced approach to agile—scrum. The following list and descriptions are not a cafeteria whereby a person can pick and choose. All of them form a system, and each part is essential. Scrum is the most widely practiced approach, and it is considered by many people to be the basis for planning and performing projects in iterations. As scrum is the most widely practiced agile framework, henceforth, we primarily use scrum language in describing ideas and techniques. When there are other widely used terms for the same thing, we will add in parentheses the additional names.

Empiricism: Work in a fact-based, experienced-based manner
Empiricism is understanding that knowledge comes from experience and making decisions based upon observable facts. Thus, plans should evolve based upon what has actually happened to date, successfully or not so successfully, and plans are firmed up only as more knowledge is identified.

Transparency: **All people present the facts as they are to create necessary trust**

Transparency means sharing all facts as they are—good, bad, or in-between in an open and timely manner. Transparency is the sharing part of information exchange, and we will see next openness is the flip side—asking for sharing. This is essential to developing trust, and trust is essential to effective collaboration. Transparency among all stakeholders leads to better trust. No one is concerned that someone else is hiding something critical only to uncover it when it is to their advantage. Trust is needed for risk-taking. This is true both for team members who want to try an unproven, but interesting approach and for decision makers who can feel confident in making significant commitments. Transparency improves decisions, as it allows for quick understanding of what is actually happening and what is working (or not). Visible and current information encourages open and honest communication among all stakeholders. Progress is based upon objective measures of working solutions. Executives like transparency, as they can see the entire work portfolio, including backlogs. Team members like transparency, as they can see the enterprise's vision and epics that summarize their work and that of other teams. All stakeholders like transparency, as they can inspect and adapt quickly and can understand the velocity of work and the amount of work in progress (WIP).

Inspection: **Everyone examines, trying to improve product, process, and people**

Everyone inspects. Workers inspect their own work, colleagues inspect each other, product owners inspect teams, other stakeholders inspect as desired. This includes inspection of both in process and final product, as well as process and people. The goal is to improve the product, process, and people.

Adaptation: **Continually improve based upon inspection**

We should all use the results of the many levels and timings of inspection to adapt and improve. We should be able to change based upon what we have discovered. Agile is sometimes called *change-driven project management*, and frequent changes both small and large are expected to continually improve. As the world is changing faster all the time, the ability to quickly adapt is a strong advantage for any organization.

Focus: **Teams finish what they start, limit work in progress (WIP)**

Remembering the ultimate users of what is being developed and the vision for how they will be satisfied helps a team develop and continue focus on work. Focus is the exact opposite of multitasking. It means assigning not just each individual, but the entire team on the highest priority work. It means making decisions sometimes based upon partial information and living with that ambiguity while discovering the fuller information. It also means finishing one thing before starting another and can mean colleagues working together to finish something quickly that ordinarily one individual might do independently but take longer.

Courage: **Tell the truth, work together, adapt to changes, question status quo, have difficult conversations**

As teams decide the best way to do work and the pace at which they can deliver, they will often find management and customers trying to demand faster or different results. Individuals at every level of the organization need to have the courage to stay firm in making decisions based upon facts and not upon demands thrust upon them. This does not give a team license to just say no, as they may often need to confront each other to find ways to get things done in a manner different than normal. Teams need courage to be prompt, transparent, and honest about progress and problems with customers and other stakeholders. They also need courage to identify personal and organizational weaknesses and to improve upon them. Teams have the courage to only focus on what is required. They will not provide excuses as they plan for success. They will stop doing something that does not work as well as needed, regardless of how much time and effort have already invested in it.

Openness: **Seek new ideas, ask for help when needed**

Related to courage, individuals need to admit when they do not know how to do something or what it is for. They need to ask for help and guidance when needed. As a team strives to improve, each member individually and the team collectively may have to consider new methods and outputs. This does not mean accepting change for the sake of change; rather, it means being open to continuing or to changing—whichever is in the best interest of the project, its customers and the team.

Commitment: **Team follows through, only take on tasks they can do**

Commitment cuts two ways. Organizational leaders must be committed to learning agile and supporting the teams that are performing. This allows and encourages experimentation and failing. Teams need to be committed. Their commitment for the medium and longer term is to the project vision—creating deliverables that are useful to their client and end-users.

Their commitment for the shorter term is to delivering what they promise during a sprint. Their commitment always is to work diligently and work to continually improve the product, process, and themselves.

Respect: **Everyone gives and feels respect, everyone contributes, team strength is collaboration, give each other permission**
All individuals must show respect for each other. When people feel respected, they will do their best work. The product owner needs to show respect for team member's ability and commitment. The scrum master needs to listen closely and develop trusting relationships with each team member. Team members need to manage conflict within their team and work toward their common goal. All parties need to stand up for each other and treat each other in a fair manner. Everyone respects themselves and each other; agreements and commitments made individually and jointly. Everyone contributes toward the common goal, and everyone has value. Developers and customers, for example, respect the expertise of each other. Management respects the rights and obligations of team members to accept responsibility. Everyone shares in the successes and failures.

Done: **Defining what acceptable will be in a sprint or release**
Knowing exactly how to evaluate deliverables to meet standards of both quality and completeness is called the definition of *done*. This explicit agreement on each deliverable portion of product ensures the developing team and product owner both understand what is being developed and how it will be used. This focuses the team on what really matters.

Extreme Programming (XP) Core Values and Practices

XP is another widely used method of agile. It has been developed and largely used for IT projects. Just as scrum pillars and values expand upon ideas that originated in the Agile Manifesto, several XP core values and practices are adaptations of the Manifesto. XP practices deal with techniques of how to do agile and will be covered in the second half of this book.

Simplicity: **Do what is needed and no more, take small simple steps, use sheerest possible design to meet today's requirement**
A basic way XP advocates describe simplicity is to say everything once and only once. To elaborate on this, everything should be stated in a clear and consistent manner with names both folks with lots of knowledge or very

little knowledge will understand and will be easy to find. There should be no duplication and no unrelated ideas grouped together. The organization should include minimal methods, classes, and couplings. Work should be created only for what is currently in use, as ideas for future enhancements may change. Design choices should be made at the last responsible moment. Finally, simplicity insists that work shall pass all tests.

Communication: **Confer on everything, every day, create best solution together**

Effective communication creates shared understanding. XP suggests sitting together to enable face-to-face communication, enhances shared understanding within a development team. When people see each other, they need to be thoughtful of both what they say and how they say it. A coach observing can facilitate improvements in communication. When a team and stakeholders jointly create user stories, they can ask each other important questions. When developers write code and documentation, they can do so incrementally, sharing often with stakeholders before finalizing. Creating, testing, and using code collectively is the most effective way to communicate.

Feedback: **Demonstrate results early, listen carefully, make adjustments**

Rapid feedback and appropriate reaction to it enables developers to write better code more quickly. XP describes feedback at multiple levels and times. The fastest feedback is between two developers who work together constantly. Next is unit testing where the smallest increment of code is immediately tested. Daily stand-up meetings provide the whole team and managers an understanding of current progress and difficulties. Acceptance testing and demonstrations give customers a chance to provide feedback after each iteration, while iteration and release planning provide feedback for weeks and months.

Lean

Lean evolved from the Toyota Production System and originally dealt with manufacturing, such as automobiles. Agile adherents found some aspects of it to be quite useful in software development. Lean thinking is the basis for the continuous flow approaches used in many agile projects. Just as the other influences, we describe some of these ideas here as being agile and others later in the book as doing agile.

*Customer-driven v*alue: **Define value from customer's perspective**

We need to consider both internal and external customers, anticipating how we can better serve them. External customers define value and determine what they will pay for. Team members find new ways to engage customers and jointly explore solutions with them. Teams attempt to deliver superior customer products and service, creating deliverables that push boundaries of what is known and deemed possible. Team members use radical hospitality and keen observation to create innovative deliverables.

Continuous improvement: **Pursue perfection by enlisting all in never-ending effort to get better**

Continuous improvement is a mindset of always striving toward perfection, and it is never ending. The intent of continuous improvement is to better focus on delivering customer value by reducing waste and optimizing processes. It includes building a culture where workers are enabled to pursue improvement opportunities. Lean thinking improves the quality of processes, people, and product. It improves the flow of work and the morale of employees. Lean thinking reduces many kinds of waste, including WIP, motion, waiting, overproduction, over processing, inconsistency, and assigning too much work to employees.

Optimize the whole **focus on what is best for entire organization**

Teams need to focus on what is best for the entire organization, including up and down the supply chain, rather than what happens to be most convenient for their team. To understand what is most value to the entire organization, teams will often find a way to visually show the flow of product and ideas from one person or group to another. This visualization helps people identify handoffs where delays and miscommunications are likely. Teams often first show the way things currently operate and then create a second flow showing how they could operate better with some changes.

Minimize work in progress (WIP): Focus on the work that has been started and finish it promptly

WIP is work that has been started but has not yet been completed. A key principle of lean is to focus on the work that has been started and finish it promptly, with as few distractions as possible. Every time a person leaves work on one item to do something else, that item is delayed. Delays mean it takes longer from the time a task is started until it is completed. As many conditions change rapidly, this increases the chance that the item being created will no longer be needed, or it will need to be changed. Also, the total amount of work accomplished over time tends to be less if people multitask, as every time a person stops one thing and starts another, that person needs to reorient their thinking to the new task.

***Minimum viable product (MVP)*: The simplest version of a product to gain quick customer feedback**

The minimum value product (MVP) is a product that can be delivered to customers for their use. The MVP is the simplest version of product that customers will want to buy. The reason for creating the simplest version first is to rapidly get something in the customer's hands and get feedback about its usefulness. If the customer likes it, then the product can be refined. If not, only a minimum amount of time and effort went into it.

PMI-ACP Exam Outline and *Agile Practice Guide*

The Project Management Institute (PMI) is by far the largest organization in the world devoted to knowledge of and advancement in project management. The PMI has evolved from an organization that primarily advocated for traditional approaches of project management, to one that recognizes different project situations call for different approaches. As such, they have started to promote agile and hybrid approaches. Three of their prongs into agile include their credential Agile Certified Practitioner (PMI-ACP), their *Agile Practice Guide* published with the Agile Alliance and distributed with the current edition of their *Guide to the Project Management Body of Knowledge (PMBOK)*, and their recent foray into Disciplined Agile. The contributions to agile in the first two of these will be covered here, and the third will have its own section later in this chapter, as it focuses on broader organizational issues.

***Advocate for agile*: Modeling agile behaviors, discussing values, and educating stakeholders**

The agile mindset is quite different than the old command-and-control style that typified at least some people's approaches to managing traditional projects. As such, it is far from enough to believe in the values of agile personally. To be successful, one needs to encourage their team, stakeholders, and their entire organization to welcome these changes. This includes modeling good agile behaviors, discussing the values including why and how they will help the organization be more effective on many projects, and educating lots of people to ensure a common understanding of agile practices and terminology. This can be especially difficult as different approaches to agile stress different aspects and use different terminology. A person promoting agile often can enjoy the power of persuasion if she or he has credibility, but seldom has the power to dictate people to change.

Establish a *shared vision*: Quickly learn desires of key stakeholders and alignment with business objectives

All projects are performed because someone or multiple individuals or groups need deliverables that the project will create. While it is hard to fully understand these needs at the outset of a project, it is possible to gain a high-level vision of what the key stakeholders wish and the tradeoffs they are willing to make. To do that, it is imperative to engage an empowered stakeholder who represents the collective opinion of stakeholders early and often so that the person can share needs and desires with the team and the team can build trust with that person. The empowered stakeholder needs to facilitate awareness among the whole range of stakeholders, so they all understand what is being created and why. The team needs to promote knowledge sharing early and often through reviews and informal means, so there is a continual flow of both information and value.

Promote *experimentation*: Encourage individuals and teams to try, perhaps fail, and share lessons

In this age of rapid change and intense competition, using the same approaches with the similar results is not good enough. Organizations and teams need to continually find ways to become more efficient and more effective. Promoting experimentation is one essential part of this improvement. The first thing managers need to do is to create a safe and trusted environment so that people feel free to experiment, fail, and share lessons from their failures, so both they and others can improve. Collaborating to share knowledge and enhance creativity go a long way toward systematic improvements. One challenge is to reduce the influence of information silos where only certain individuals or groups have access to useful information. The answer to that sharing is not to inundate people with more correspondences than they already wade through, but to share information targeted to those who can use it and to provide access to as full of information as possible to any stakeholder who requires it. Teams need to work with managers to gain (develop?) dedicated members and letting them know they will be on a team for long term. This would motivate them to improve. Also, teams need to ensure that all members' ideas are valued and considered.

Encourage *emergent leadership:* Create safe environment where team members promote each other into influential opportunities

Emergent leadership is bottom-up. This is in sharp contrast to a command-and-control style. To successfully encourage emergent leadership, an organization must create a safe and respectful environment where self-organizing and empowerment are not threatened. Then workers feel safe in sharing incomplete thoughts, knowing that better ideas are developed jointly. It often takes effort to ensure all workers are engaged, as some are accustomed to being told what to do and how to do it. Different projects may require different amounts of semistructure to enable local and flexible organizing. Team members increasingly depend on each other and agree on their approach to work developing working agreements and ground rules if needed. The team collectively decides what work will be done and who will do what at each time. They can do this because they have or can develop the needed skills. Team members develop the ability to have constructive dialogue and often meet and make decisions with no manages present.

Practice *servant leadership:* Person in authority's primary role is to help others perform better

Servant leadership can be practiced in many situations, not just agile projects. It really is revolutionary to many people, as it starts with inspiring others through the project vision and with the notion that a leader is a servant first. Servant leaders view projects as creating something for the common good. The leader has a primary desire to help others. The help can include many things such as:

- Promoting sense of community
- Helping others grow into more autonomous and wise people
- Listening for understanding and empathy

- Coaching
- Help teams collaborate
- Manage relationships
- Facilitate coordination
- Remove impediments
- Educate stakeholders
- Promoting safety, respect, trust, and so on

Some servant leaders are visionary, vividly describing lofty project goals. Others may not have that gift, but still communicate visions to others to establish, sustain movement toward that vision, and guide teams to make wise decisions.

Scaled Agile Framework (SAFe) Core Values

SAFe is both a philosophy and set of tools designed to synchronize alignment of multiple teams within large enterprises by having organizational leaders creating broad frameworks, collaborating with them, and assisting in their delivery. SAFe draws primarily from agile, lean, and systems thinking. The four SAFe core values described as follows bring much of the systems thinking to bear.

Alignment on enterprise business objectives supported by clear lines of authority

Organizational leaders use alignment to empower teams and do not use coercive command-and-control methods. Rather, they strive toward twin goals that are aimed to decentralize decision making, while at the same time, coordinating multiple teams through synchronization. Leaders set strategy at the enterprise level. They model what they want teams to do at the portfolio level. That is, using customer understanding and relationships and design thinking, create a vision to work toward and a backlog of possible work that may help achieve that vision. These enterprise leaders then cascade this down through ongoing programs and to individual agile teams. They establish clear lines of authority and describe objectives and goals. Individual teams maintain a cadence of work by setting and using team routines. All of this is flexible, as leaders know variability exists and options need to be considered.

Built-in quality ensuring every element and every increment reflect quality standards

Built-in quality is emphasized in SAFe as larger and more complex systems present more opportunities for problems and a higher need to ensure quality through good practices. Built-in quality has multiple advantages. It is needed for predictability and velocity, as teams need to count on the quality of every aspect of a system. Built-in quality helps to avoid costly delays and minimize WIP. It helps optimize systems through building products on stable bases so that change and compliance are easier. It results in higher customer satisfaction and better system performance. Many different practices from various agile approaches can be used. Five aspects of quality are enhanced:

1. Flow quality: By using a test-first mentality with simplified tests and conducted early in the process to remove errors, rework, and waste.
2. Architecture and design quality: By considering future needs, evaluating options before deciding, creating good coupling between parts, and using sensible naming conventions.
3. Code quality: By testing and documenting each part, including edge cases and boundary conditions.
4. System quality: By creating a shared understanding of exactly how each feature should perform and continually testing the integration of each into the system.
5. Release: By using modular architecture to allow small releases that business users can evaluate, ensuring compliance by proving the system meets its intended use with no adverse consequences, and scaling the definition of done from small stories through entire systems.

Program execution providing intense focus on working systems and business outcomes

The core value of excellent program execution is made easier if the organization is successful applying the first three core values of alignment, built-in quality, and transparency. The organization continuously delivers working systems and business value through incremental solutions focusing on value, reliability, and efficiency. Organizations often create an Agile Release Team (ART), which is a team of teams and other individuals who operate for the long haul. The ART coordinates the work of various teams using design thinking and ensuring a continual pipeline of useful working product. The ART maintains and communicates a higher-level perspective of how each team and their outputs fit. The enterprise needs to reduce the impact of information silos, become more cross-functional, and establish effective working agreements.

Disciplined Agile

Disciplined Agile is an all-inclusive system of multiple aspect that includes updates to the manifesto, principles, promises, guidelines, beliefs, role definitions, lifecycles, and governance milestones. We first briefly cover several of the Manifesto updates. These updates clarify and expand upon some of the ideas in the original Manifesto. While consistent with the original intent, they attempt to ensure more complete solutions. As with the original Manifesto, the emphasis is on the terms on the left of each set, but the terms on the right are not ignored.

Then, we cover multiple ideas from the other aspects that pertain to the agile mindset and are not already mentioned in preceding sections. We cover the parts of Disciplined Agile that are more technique-oriented, including lifecycle and governance milestones in Chapter 6.

Disciplined Agile Manifesto Updates

Solutions deliverables that are usable, desirable, and functional in helping customers achieve desired outcomes
This goes beyond the original Manifesto idea of delivering software that worked. It includes necessary documentation and understanding of business processes. The solutions need to be workable and desirable. The ultimate goal is to enable customers to use the outputs of the project to successfully achieve their aims.

Stakeholders, not just customers
This section is consistent with the ideas many people have expressed in recent years. A project team needs to consider the myriad of stakeholders who have some sort of interest in and/or power over a project. While the original Manifesto may have implied that, by using the term customer, some people interpreted that as primarily delivering customer value to

end users. The broader stakeholder view also requires delivering broader business value to the organization.

Teams, not projects

Agile teams ideally stay together for a long period of time. Projects can be considered to be temporary. Also, some agile projects are cut short when decision makers decide either there is enough capability and some original functionality is not needed or maybe the entire idea is scrapped. The team can still stay together and can work on the next project or set of functionality. So much of the organizing and leadership is related to the team, that focus on the team instead of the project makes sense.

Organizations, not just teams

A single team can make improvements by understanding many of the agile mindset ideas and practicing many of the agile methods. However, to gain truly outsized improvements, the entire organization needs to embrace and adopt agile. There are so many ways an organization that does not support agile can undermine good intentions of a team. Advocating for agile, as described previously, can help many people in the broader organization understand and value agile.

Feedback, not just change

Agile teams need to be flexible and will often change, sometimes dramatically. The changes do not just happen. They happen in response to rapid and continual feedback from engaged stakeholders. As stakeholders see and use early deliverables, they increasingly describe what they like and what they do not like. Thus, through extensive feedback, the true and complete requirements gradually emerge. This continual monitoring is more effective and timely than periodic reviews.

Measure outcomes, not just deliverables

Each team needs to understand the outcomes that users of their deliverables are seeking. These outcomes should drive assessment. This emphasis on helping users achieve success requires a deeper understanding of user situations and needs than the old view of creating agreed-upon deliverables and thinking that is good enough. This outcomes emphasis demands establishing a longer-term relationship with stakeholders, not a temporary transaction mentality.

Transparency over false predictability

Organizational leaders work collaboratively with agile teams. This enhances transparency in two ways. Teams are more aware of broader organizational issues and actions of other teams and the organizational leaders know more about what the team is doing. The team starts with high-level planning early in the process. They record important events and processes in real time using a system that will allow insight. The team encourages stakeholders to visit on-site and view information as it is created. The team uses simple milestones that can indicate when risks are overcome. Organizational leaders create simple systems making it easy for teams to do work in the preferred manner.

Disciplined Agile Principles, Promises, Guidelines, and Beliefs

We cover just the few items from these areas that Disciplined Agile stresses in more detail than other agile approaches do. There are many more items in these lists.

Delight customers

This goes beyond the Manifesto's first two points of customer being highest priority and being willing to change even late for the benefit of the customer. We want to surprise the customer with a solution to their problem beyond their expectations. We want to help create a solution for the customer that is easier for them to use, faster, and helps them get the exact information when they want it in a form they can use.

Be awesome

As leaders, we want to earn respect and trust of co-workers and other stakeholders. We do this by being honest, collaborative learners. We grant teams authority and needed resources so that they can serve their customers very well. We want the workers in our agile teams to feel special and be thrilled they are working with us.

Be pragmatic

Our goal is to be effective, not to be a slave to one particular methodology. Each organization, project, and individual is different, and so, we do not expect to use a *one-size-fits-all* model. Many teams will decide to use some sort of hybrid approach drawing from two different agile approaches or even part agile and part traditional. The point is to use whatever framework that makes the most sense, given your organization and the specifics of your project.

Context counts and choice is good

Collectively, these two concepts carry the be pragmatic goal by encouraging teams to recognize the situation their project and organization are in and to choose the lifecycle model and methods they will use. The size of a team and the needs of a project will help a team decide what agile aspects they will use and how they will tailor them.

Organize around products and services

Instead of organizing by functional areas, we want to organize around our customers. We focus on the value stream of processes and decisions that impact a customer with an eye toward delighting them. This product focus enables team members to focus on what their customers value, so they can focus on producing exactly that.

Enterprise awareness

We want all of our workers to see the big picture of our organization. We do not want to suboptimize by having each team do what is best for them, regardless of the impact it may have on others. We share transparently as we all work toward organizational goals.

Create psychological safety and embrace diversity

If we are to truly create situations in which teams self-organize, all members need to feel safe in being themselves. We value the great variety of people with the different thoughts and ideas each brings from their eclectic perspectives. We treat each other with respect and expect respect in turn. We use role clarity and give people the opportunity to perform meaningful work.

Create semiautonomous self-organizing teams

We wish to staff our teams with generalizing specialists who are expert at one or more things and have some working knowledge of others. We encourage our team members to continue to learn a variety of different things that may help. By having a wider variety of both expert and working knowledge among team members, there is less need for formal documentation (although we still need some). We understand that it is often impractical to fully staff a team, so our team will need to interact with others.

Complexity belief

As we perform our projects, we will often need to solve complex, adaptive problems. By the mere act of working on these problems, we often change the problem itself. Many of these problems have far-reaching consequences, and we cannot know all of the possible ramifications of our actions in advance.

Architecture owner

One role specified in Disciplined Agile is that of an architecture owner. This is the lead technical person on a project, often the senior developer. This person leads in a facilitating manner, but has ultimate decision-making authority on technical issues and is accountable for integrating the team's work products into organizational systems. While the product owner wants to have the right product created and the team lead wants to build quickly, the architecture owner wants to make sure the work is done properly.

Summary of Key Ideas in the Mindset

This chapter has briefly summarized key agile mindset ideas first from the Agile Manifesto and then enhancements to that seminal document that are espoused by multiple agile streams. These include scrum, XP, lean, PMI's Exam Outline, and *Agile Practice Guide*, SAFe, and Disciplined Agile Manifesto. While there is a significant overlap between what the various approaches suggest, we highlighted a few thoughts that each approach emphasizes, either more or differently than others and that contribute to the rich system of thinking that is the mindset of being agile.

The total of this might seem bewildering, especially because some of the approaches use different terminology for similar ideas. For that reason, we summarize next how all of these ideas fit into a systematic approach, and then, in the next three chapters, we delve into each of the three major sections in more depth.

Successful Outcomes

- Customer-driven vision
- Customer-driven value
- Simplicity
- Excellence
- Improvement

Project success is now viewed more comprehensively than in the past. A thorough understanding of what one is trying to accomplish on a project leads to the behaviors and processes that will achieve it. We view project success from the standpoint of the project vision, understanding stakeholders, and delivering value. The vision of a project is aligned with organizational goals and is used to inspire. Agile places great emphasis on understanding and developing strong relationships with the whole myriad of stakeholders. A commitment to delivering value early and continuously is the core of agile.

When we do these things well, we deliver superior products. One key is simplicity—doing only what is needed and making it in a clear, consistent, and understandable manner. When we practice excellence in all of our activities, quality goes up and stakeholders are more pleased. Agile teams reflect often on what works and what does not work in an effort to improve products, people, and processes.

Project success is possible by delivering value incrementally, evaluating the value, and then work on more functional values. Success is not a goal; it is a journey.

Engaging Your Team

- Leadership
- Motivation
- Decision making

Projects are conducted with and for people. Agile is the anti-thesis for command and control. The changes required for servant and emergent leadership are fundamental and require a true belief that workers are thinking, caring individuals who are capable of making great decisions and accomplishing great things. Showing respect to all team members, understanding their motivations, and capitalizing on both their individual and team strengths demand an unleashing of control. Helping team members make decisions rather than making decisions for them is a hallmark of agile. The goal is to develop self-managed teams and provide coaching and leadership support as and when necessary.

Effective Communication and Collaboration

- Transparency
- Feed back
- Timeliness

Greatly improved communication is both a goal of agile and a means to help it to be effective. Transparency in communication drives trust and better decisions. Sharing preliminary ideas and partial work allows stakeholders to provide rapid feedback, which, in turn, allows rapid changes and improvements. Projects are often under great time pressure and having effective communication, when it is helpful to make progress and to make good decisions, adds greatly to project success. For this purpose, agile project teams are colocated to enhance frequent and effective communication and client representatives work with projects teams constantly and frequently interact with the team to improve communication.

The next three chapters expand upon these three aspects of being agile—the broad understanding of project success, leadership and teamwork requirements, and effective communication. The second half of the book considers the mechanics of *doing agile* again with advice from various streams of agile, combining them into a coherent whole. We summarize these many ideas into the three topics of:

1. Planning adaptively
2. Creating useful solutions
3. Giving and using feedback

Summary

Appreciating the agile mindset requires understanding Agile Manifesto principles, the basis for various agile streams. This agile mindset requires a fundamental understanding of agile streams such as scrum, extreme programming, lean, PMI ACP, SAFe, and Disciplined Agile. Core values and principles of all these agile streams vary, and these differences are subtle and sometimes not so subtle. All these agile streams are briefly discussed in this chapter along with PMI ACP certificate guidelines on these concepts. It is important to have a big picture and a common understanding of all these agile streams, and for this purpose, an agile model is proposed for a better perspective of the key factors and associated elements. Each key factor is essential to manage agile projects effectively and efficiently.

Questions

1. Agile values and Agile Manifesto principles are the foundations of the agile method. How are they, and to what extent are they adapted by various agile streams discussed in this chapter?
2. Of the agile streams discussed in this chapter, which one is applicable for what type of project?
3. Please discuss the benefits and challenges associated with all the agile streams. If you are asked to pick one, which one will you select and why?

CHAPTER 3

Successful Outcomes

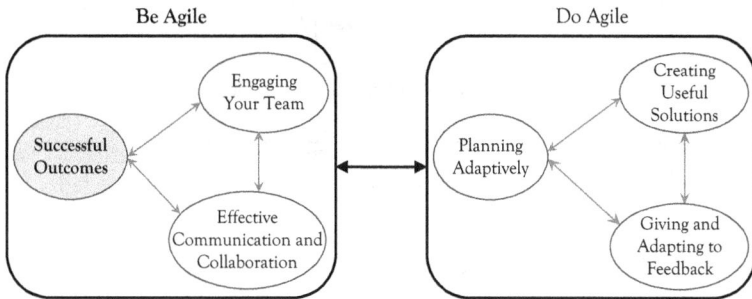

This is the first of three chapters that collectively describe *being agile*. These chapters include many concepts that form the core of understanding how we need to view agile projects and people working in them. When we need to define a tool or metric that is part of *doing agile* to fully describe a concept, we will do so briefly in a textbox and then cover it more fully in the second half of this book.

After reading this chapter, you will be able to:

1. Develop a customer focus to define vision and value for a project
2. Understand important aspects of simplicity, excellence, and improvement in developing the product for your agile project

There are five key drivers of successful outcomes in agile projects, as shown in Figure 3.1. Note they are all interrelated—all are important.

Consistently delivering excellent value to clients is a goal of any organization, whether they use agile or not. One needs to understand a vision for the products they are creating and how customers value them.

The three key aspects of superior sustainable delivery: namely simplicity, excellence, and continuous improvement depend on understanding

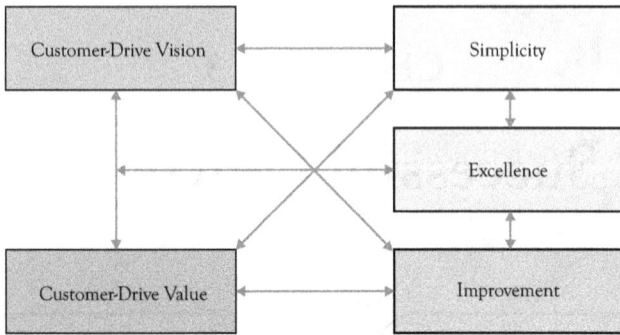

Figure 3.1 ***Drivers of successful outcomes from agile***

and working toward a project vision that customers value. A key aspect of any approach to agile is simplicity: doing only what is needed and no more, working lean, using the simplest design that will perform as needed, and working in a sustainable manner. A second key aspect is excellence in all things: attention to detail, everyone inspects, striving for personal excellence, and reducing technical debt. The third aspect is continuous improvement: a constant effort to improve people, process, and product by allowing people to experiment and adapt.

Customer-Driven Vision

A *product vision* describes customer satisfaction and alignment with business objectives at an initially high level. The first consideration for a product vision is to remember that customer satisfaction is the highest priority. The very reason for performing any project is to create a product, service, or change that someone or some group(s) need to do their work. The vision is to satisfy the customer(s) above all else. That means the old iron triangle of trading off cost, schedule, and scope may not always apply directly. The agile way of looking at things is—we create useful products for customers and the specifics of cost, schedule, and scope may vary—as long as the tradeoffs are made to better satisfy the customer.

When considering the customer, it is best to consider the entire supply chain. Often, the person or group that a development team meets most may be the next in line, but not always the ultimate user. Also, we need to look backward in the supply chain to understand how our suppliers are creating products and services we need to do our work. We may need to share an understanding of the product vision with our suppliers.

The product vision should be aligned with enterprise business objectives. Yes, we need to keep the end user in mind, but we also need to keep in mind how our work fits with all of the other work and strategy of the organization. Strategy is set at the enterprise level and translated into a portfolio of projects and other work. This portfolio view is useful in empowering teams, as members will have relevant and important information to understand and can make more informed decisions at their level. Executives can have confidence that they can better coordinate the work of multiple teams as everyone has a common understanding of where their work fits. This coordination can be supported by clear lines of authority linked to objectives and goals.

An empowered stakeholder may be the person who shares the original vision with the development team. This vision typically is only described at a high level early along with tradeoffs the business is willing to make. This helps all stakeholders to understand what is to be created and why.

One way to describe a product vision, long before technical specifications make sense, is to create a *metaphor*. A metaphor compares two seemingly different things in such a manner that key similarities are emphasized. By describing the output needs of a project using a surprising comparison, team members can grasp why this work is being done and then develop a common language. For example, if one is creating a small arboretum, perhaps it could be described as a small tree library. Then people know you want a collection of different tree species. You want them identified easily with signs and probably want an app to let people take a picture of each sign so that they can immediately get more information. However, as it is a small library, you will have a limited number of species and limited space. This metaphor helps everyone involved understand what you are trying to accomplish, and before you develop detailed specifications, you can still make many decisions.

Customer-Driven Value

There are four components to the expected value when successfully using agile on any project:

1. Because of the collaboration and transparent and continuous communication, which we describe later in this book, all stakeholders

have more visibility into the current status of the project, including any potential problems.

2. Risk is rapidly reduced. While any good approach to project management identifies potential risks and comes up with plans to address the major risks, agile goes a big step further. When a major risk is identified, other work is frequently postponed until that risk can be reduced or eliminated. Risk is considered to be anti-value and is dealt with directly and quickly.

3. Agile projects retain significant adaptability throughout their life. They do this by only making commitments that are needed for the immediate work that is being done. Detailed specifications and locked-in decisions are put off until the last responsible moment. Change that benefits the customer is eagerly accepted, even late in the project.

4. An agile saying is "eat your desert first." I do not tell this to my grandkids. The idea behind this saying is, work on the thing that will give maximum value first. That may be eliminating the biggest risk as that is anti-value or creating the most enticing feature. Clients benefit from using the new thing right away and often become strong advocates for your project.

To define value from the customer's perspective on your specific project, you might invite key stakeholders to your planning meetings. They can describe what they want, why it is important, and if they are paying customers, what they will pay for. Business value is often described in financial terms, helping developers understand which portions of potential project work are more vital.

Value may be considered differently at different times in a project. Ultimately, agile emphasizes that value is determined by outcomes, not by outputs. That means understanding how a user will use the outputs and how those outputs will contribute to their success is essential. A relationship view of dealing with customers is needed for this to happen, rather than merely a transactional view of "this is the specification you requested, and it is what I am delivering." Customers do not always know at the outset what they need, but they do understand how their success will be judged. The best agile teams learn from their customers and create products and services that help their customers to be successful.

During the project, value is determined by how quickly useful products and services are delivered so that the customer can begin to have an early return on their investment. By receiving useful bits of product early and often, clients can give rapid feedback on what they like and do not like, what helps them and what does not, and so on. This enables teams to prioritize work based upon what customers value. As decisions are made, documentation follows. That is superior to the old way of creating extensive documentation first, seeing what clients valued in product that was delivered, and then having to do rework, as some of the early documentation forced teams to create less valuable products.

Simplicity

There are several agile approaches that are designed to be efficient and effective. They are focused on:

- Executing only what needs to be done
- Working lean by defining process and sticking to it
- Defining done
- Maximizing work not done
- Focusing on the simplest possible design to meet today's requirements
- Refining the *product backlog*
- Working at pace that team can sustain

Product backlog A wish list of things that may be created by the project team

Doing things as simply as one can and yet be effective is one hallmark of agile, regardless of the variant of the agile approach used. Part of that is to work only what is needed and no more. Of course, this requires judgment to decide what is truly needed. Part of that judgment should stem from the very definition of product success—what does your customer value? Doing just enough means doing just enough documentation. Initially, that may be fairly simple, but as decisions are made firmly, documentation is increased to whatever extent is needed. Part of doing just enough can be envisioned as decluttering and deduplicating. Part of it is firmly saying no to extraneous requirements. Doing only what is needed can be implemented by using the 80/20 principle. Twenty percent of the possible functions and features can often yield 80 percent of the value, so start by identifying those 20 percent and do them. If more is needed later, more can be added then.

An aspect of simplicity is working lean. *Lean* means eliminating waste of any kind. By eliminating waste, no extra motion, no extra waiting, no extra work, and no rework on unneeded product is performed. To the extent possible, once work is started on one thing, it is followed through to completion, so there is no partially completed work clogging up the system and waiting for a worker to restart it. Another type of waste is defective work. Doing things simply as described earlier, with a defined process as described next, and using an improvement mindset, as described later in this chapter help to reduce defective work.

Working lean is accomplished by defining a process to create the product and both sticking to it and improving it. Ideally, the process is defined using small, simple steps. Progressive elaboration allows workers to start with simple steps on their simple product and add just enough complexity as users begin to demand as they use the emerging product and test its potential. When using a *time-box* version of agile, details are frozen for the current iteration. This allows a process to be followed. User stories are decomposed into small, actionable steps.

Time-box defines the start and stop times for the agreed amount of work to be performed.

Another agile concept that enhances simplicity is the definition of *done*. This means the developers and the product owner agree before work starts on exactly how a product increment will be judged; who will test it, under what circumstances, and to what level must it perform to be considered done. Knowing exactly what the *product increment* must do allows developers to create exactly that and no more, using a lean, defined process.

Product increment: The deliverables created and accepted during a sprint

Sprint (aka: increment) Short period when committed to deliverables are created

An important agile simplicity concept is maximizing the work not done. One way to maximize work not done is to deliver value at each sprint. Also, developers and product owners often agree on what constitutes the minimum viable product (MVP). The MVP is a product increment that is complete enough to be useful as is to end-users. It is often a plain vanilla version of something that may be later enhanced. One approach to determining the MVP is to ask users what are the three to five features that would give them the most business value. By delivering value during each increment and focusing on the MVP, if priorities change and work needs to be halted, the users still have something useful. Many agile teams celebrate when something is not needed as that helps maximize work not done.

Simplicity also suggests using the simplest possible design to meet today's requirements, knowing future requirements may change. What looks like something that may be requested, may not, and something completely unforeseen may emerge.

Product backlog refining helps to simplify. By breaking large backlog items into small, understandable pieces, development work can be easily envisioned. Better-defined backlog items are easier to estimate and deliver.

Product backlog refining: Understand, slice, and estimate time to create user stories.

A final simplicity idea is to work at a pace the team can sustain. Planning and maintaining to the extent possible a 40-hour work week makes long-term work sustainable.

Excellence

Each person involved individually, and as a team, strives for excellence. Everyone inspects—their own work as well as any other work.

Attention to technical excellence and good design yield the best results. For a good design, a solution should be usable, desirable, and functional. An ideal design is the one that is straightforward, includes no more detail than needed, and is understandable enough both to serve as a basis for work and to change. Designs often need to be updated as more work is included, and users provide feedback.

Refactoring is a term that means continually asking; does every part of the product we are developing work well together? Are there duplications that can be reduced? Do all of the parts seamlessly interface with each other? Is the design as efficient as possible?

Refactoring: Simplifying and cleaning product to make it stable and maintainable.

There are various means to determine excellence. One way is to ask questions such as, was good product shipped and accepted by the customer? After the work was completed, did the leadership and team stay intact (or possibly get promoted)? After evaluating their process and results, would the team perform the same way again, potentially with just a few improvements? If the results were good and the team would stay intact and work essentially as the same team again, then excellence was achieved.

Improvement

A goal of agile is to simultaneously improve people, process, communication, and product. Teams use continuous process improvement, recognizing that small improvements add up. Quality, efficiency, and effectiveness can all be enhanced.

Encouraging fast failure is a hallmark of agile. That means people are allowed and encouraged to experiment, know that not every experiment will yield improvements. However, experiments that do not, still yield learning. Experimenting and quickly failing promote innovation and reduce rework.

Knowledge sharing is a big part of agile, and indeed, for any effective work environment. Teams self-assess to learn what works well and what can be improved. Teams generally try to improve one thing at a time and then reflect on it. Teams share internally between members and externally with other teams. However, these lessons learned are not mandated for other teams because of the recognition that what works for one team may not work for another team. A good reason to reflect is that tacit knowledge is often the most impactful kind. Tacit knowledge is not formally documented, but still helps people to improve. Related to gathering knowledge is problem-solving. The most effective teams have everyone actively involved in solving problems and then reflecting on their success.

Teams adapt. They continually improve based upon results, both those that are discovered through inspection and those uncovered through reflection. Adaptation may be minor, merely tweaking something to be a bit better. Adaptation may also be major, pivoting immediately after an iteration either because the customer wants something different or the team understands a better way.

Agile uses empiricism instead of strict plans. That means work is conducted in a fact-based manner. Empiricism is a belief that knowledge comes from experience. Therefore, agile teams make decisions based upon what has worked and not on a detailed plan that was developed at the outset of the project. One term sometimes used in agile thinking is *yesterday's weather*. Common wisdom suggests the best single factor to predict today's weather is what happened yesterday. In the same way, the best single factor teams use in adapting their plans is what worked so far. Of course, like weather forecasts, more than one factor is often used to create good agile plans.

Agile often uses what are called collaboration games (sometimes known as innovation games) to promote innovation and improvement. A variety of these games and variations of each exist. The informal nature of these games helps team members feel safe in proposing unproven ideas. Essentially what they all strive to do is facilitate discussion among team members regarding what they might do in the future. Some of these games encourage team members to visualize the future and speculate on what happened and why. Some look at what has been done to date and speculate on what might be the next things to do and what the advantages and disadvantages of each alternative are. Once the teams do this speculation with whatever collaboration game they use, they often become more innovative on their plans.

Summary

This chapter presents concepts of simplicity, excellence, and improvement that are driven by customer-driven vision and value. The key issue is that customers do not always know what they need at the outset, but they do understand how their success will be judged. This subtle difference must be understood well for developing successful outcomes. The vision must be aligned with an organization's objectives and goals. Integral to the vision is understanding stakeholders and their needs and delivering value to all the stakeholders. Simplicity is focused on work that is absolutely necessary to avoid unnecessary work and rework. When a team focuses on excellence, it provides value to all the key stakeholders that results in high-quality deliverable that is of value to the customer. The aim is always to improve products, processes, communication, and people continuously.

Questions

1. How do you develop customer-driven vision and value for a project?
2. Please explain in detail how you would incorporate aspects of simplicity, excellence, and improvement in developing the product for your agile project?

CHAPTER 4

Engaging Your Team: Leadership, Teamwork, and Roles

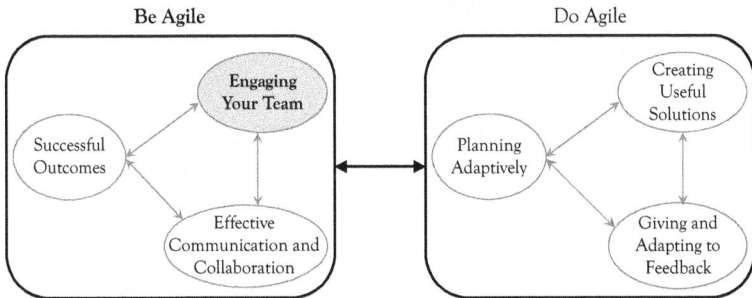

Be Agile   Do Agile

```
Engaging Your Team

Successful Outcomes

Effective Communication and Collaboration

Planning Adaptively

Creating Useful Solutions

Giving and Adapting to Feedback
```

As previously discussed, the global economy is here to stay largely because of the drastic growth of information and communication technologies (ICT). Associated with the global economy is open market philosophy, and together, they trigger significant rise in market demand and competition. Organizations are left with no option but to extend products and services faster, better, and cheaper. This is where project teams play a critical role as they are responsible for development and delivery of products and services and accountable for doing them efficiently and effectively. The agile method took shape under these circumstances, and project teams did not have the luxury to go through the traditional stages of group development. For many projects, project teams employed rapid iterative cycles to perform at a high level immediately after the team is formed.

After reading this chapter, you will be able to:

1. Describe the pros and cons of servant and emergent leadership for agile projects and how are they suited in your agile project.
2. Describe the team development model proposed in the chapter and tell why or why not you feel it is appropriate.
3. Describe primary and additional team roles and responsibilities typical on agile projects.

For any project, a group of individuals are assembled together to form a team and to deliver the project outcomes. Generally, a project team comprises of individuals representing multiple disciplines with complementary skills. Project teams typically outperform individual efforts because project tasks require collaborative work to make the best use of diverse skills, experience, and judgment. Also, project team size varies considerably and is driven by the project characteristics such as scope, complexity, and diverse and complimentary skill sets necessary to develop project deliverables. A project team's ability to demonstrate cohesiveness and synergy is critical because of the interdependent nature of tasks and coordination among team members to deliver the project outcomes successfully.

Project teams can function in different types; teams can be colocated, virtual, global, or a combination of these three types. Virtual teams are those that communicate using technology, and they may be colocated, or geographically dispersed either nationally or internationally. Global project teams are often set up as virtual teams where team members are dispersed geographically across national boundaries. The type of team formation influences cohesion, communication, and collaboration. Leadership style is also influenced by these three types of teams. Obviously, the project manager will have to adapt different styles of leadership for different types of teams.

Global business units often have global projects comprised of individual rollout projects in each region of the world being coordinated with an overall global timeline. An example is implementing a new SAP demand planning application in Asia, Latin America, Europe, and North America for Procter and Gamble businesses. Therefore, one must understand the global business environment, relevant cultures, legal and political environment of the host nation.

Project team size and composition vary for traditional and agile projects, as their approach, circumstances, and issues are different. Specifically, agile project teams use rolling-wave planning to refine the deliverables as they move forward and estimate their costs, which is not the case for traditional projects. Agile project characteristics demand a project team that is unconventional and different from a traditional project team. The agile project team interacts with the client frequently, and in many situations, the client becomes a member of the agile team. Agile project teams are set up as small and colocated (when practical) teams to manage rapid changes and incremental functions to the scope. The team should be receptive, flexible, and responsive to client's requirements. Needless to say, agile teams require a higher commitment and greater collaboration from team members, as uncertainties and changes are the norm for agile projects. Issues of uncertainty and frequent changes in functional requirements foster tactics that focus on flow and value generation, action perspective for execution, and scientific experimentation model for control.

So, how do all these translate into operational strategies for the team? While working collaboratively, the agile project team members, simultaneously, are presumed to be independent. Also, these client requirements envisage people working on agile projects to be inherently motivated. Consequent to this fluid situation and operational strategies, agile teams must be prepared to assume simplicity, accept change, maximize value, and offer frequent and speedy feedback to all stakeholders. Agile team members are encouraged to question everything, innovate, propose, and implement incremental changes and deliver value frequently (Kloppenborg, Anantatmula and Wells 2018).

Leadership

Four leadership styles are prominently discussed in the management literature and research studies. They are transactional, transformational, emergent, and servant leadership styles, of which the last two styles assume greater importance from the agile perspective. In general, applicability of these leadership styles would depend on many organizational factors such as culture, project at hand, availability of resources, and urgency of the work.

Table 4.1 Leadership styles and their value in agile

Style	Characteristics	Value in agile
Transactional	Leader with position authority uses rewards and punishment to gain compliance.	Counter-productive.
Transformational	Leader aims to develop trust and align personal values of individuals (followers) to accomplish vision and mission of the organization.	Motivates team members to work toward project vision.
Servant	Leader focuses on needs of the followers first through integrating followers needs with project goals, honesty, delegation, and empowerment.	Allows team members to grow and to focus on their work with few distractions.
Emergent	Scrum masters, product owners, and coaches encourage team members to lead.	With more people taking the leadership role, the bias for action speeds work and encourages collaboration.

Transactional Leadership

In *transactional leadership* style, a leader identifies and acknowledges needs of the followers first, and then sets up an exchange process to meet them in a way that is beneficial to both the leader and the follower. Transactional leadership is based on position authority that is assigned because of the hierarchical position in the organization structure. This style of leadership is applied for task completion using rewards and punishments. This might have been in vogue in the past but will be not for many organizations in the current knowledge economy wherein many employees are educated and possess specialized skills.

Transformational Leadership

Transformational leadership style aims to reconstruct personal values of individuals (followers) to accomplish vision and mission of the organization. This transformation is possible only when trust is established. And, trust is possible if the leader is respected and emulated. However, shared vision is possible when individual aspirations are aligned with organizational values and goals. Consequently, another important attribute of transformational leader is the ability to motivate followers through intellectual stimulation and personal attention to everyone in the team. This works well in many organizations where traditional project management practices are employed. This leadership style may also work in many agile project environments.

In an organization where traditional or plan-driven projects are the norm, transformational leadership fits better. Why? Any project is conceived to operationalize strategic objectives of an organization. A transformational leader emphasis is placed on the organization and its objectives. A transformation leader motivates their team to develop commitment for the organizational objectives. However, the agile project team leadership may prefer a different approach. Team and team member development is of paramount importance, and the servant and emergent leadership styles may be preferred.

Servant Leadership

Servant leadership style takes the position that a leader must focus on needs of the followers first. A key focus of the servant leadership is appreciation of the followers. Honesty, integration, delegation, and empowerment are important attributes in servant leadership. Servant leadership style is gaining popularity in many industries, as delegation and empowerment are considered important, specifically for many Gen X and Y professionals. Obviously, it is gaining popularity with agile project management teams comprising of highly qualified and technical professionals.

Transformational and servant leaderships are similar in terms of vision, trust, delegation, empowerment, and influence on followers. The main difference between transformational leadership and servant leadership is the emphasis the leader places with the team. Transformational leaders focus first on the goals and secondarily on the team. Servant leader focus is on service to their followers and is suitable for agile projects where people with similar levels of expertise and experience work together.

A servant leader keeps her main focus on followers, while accomplishing organizational objectives is of secondary importance.

In the servant leadership style, it is okay to assign secondary importance to organizational objectives as agile team members are usually highly qualified, self-motivated, and committed to the job. So, they must be nurtured, and servant leadership style works very well in this case. A servant leader takes the approach of leading as a facilitator and not as a person who adapts the command-and-control approach. In this leadership style, the servant leader will work with team members to collaborate daily, ensure team growth, protect team from distractions, and guide through coaching.

It is a critical role of the servant leader to provide guidance as a coach of the team. For this to happen, the leader must establish both informal and formal communication channels that are effective. She or he should listen to all the team members attentively while treating them with respect and dignity. Furthermore, the team should be allowed to work autonomously and must be empowered to make decisions. This level of functional freedom comes with accountability and trust. The leader must be well versed with technical, administrative, and organizational-related legal issues to function effectively.

Emergent Leadership

Another form of leadership that is gaining popularity among agile projects is emergent leadership. *Emergent leadership* is often informal—with different team members taking on leadership roles at different times. This type of leadership is formed when team members perceive someone as an influential in the team. Self-organizing teams need leadership from many individuals. There is no project manager who performs all of the facilitation and coordination. Scrum masters and product owners do some of that, but some is still required from team members. Team member active involvement is a strong predictor of success. Emergent leadership is building from within a team and with those members who especially support the team and organization's core values.

The entire concept of emergent leadership is that leaders are both self-selected and encouraged by their peers much more than they are selected by an external formal authority. As agile team members are generalized specialists, each has strong expertise in something. One hopes that at least some of these team members exert themselves in the areas they know well.

Team members, scrum masters, product owners, and agile coaches can all encourage team members to lead by being on the lookout for team members who can lead in certain situations, who have a bias for action, and who actively practice team and organizational values.

Effective agile teams balance team autonomy with organizational alignment. Team members tend to be most engaged and active if they feel they can control much of their own destiny. However, the team still needs to support the overall organization and the product vision of the customer. Those in formal leadership positions such as product owners, scrum masters, and agile coaches encourage leadership from team members. One way to provide this encouragement is to enunciate and act consistently with their values and expect others to do the same. Leading with values keeps teams aligned but gives them the freedom to figure out how they will accomplish their work. This is a more active leadership role than doing nothing and expecting good results and a less active leadership role than micromanaging. Trust, transparency, and flexibility are also conditions that encourage leaders to emerge.

Emerging leaders display core values of team and organization. They are big on collaboration and cooperation. Emergent leaders carefully observe and listen to their teammates. They surface conflict and strive to create an atmosphere where all team members feel safe to engage in helpful discussion and debate.

Emergent leadership promotes individual, team, and organizational growth and improvement.

Team members are motivated, have fun, are productive. Teams find better ways of working and place more emphasis on adding value.

Leading Agile Project Teams

Many factors affect the success of a project team such as leadership, role definition, delegation, conflict resolution, and change orientation impact project success (Rogers and Anantatmula 2018). Project managers must be able to adapt to "both traditional and agile tools, techniques, and methods for each project" (PMBOK 2017; p. 58). However, we contend that both the project team and the project manager must adapt to the project management method as it influences functioning styles of them alike. The necessity, for project managers is to tailor application of traditional and agile practices to meet project needs, emphasize the importance of understanding the similarities and differences between traditional and agile project teams, and make the necessary adjustments to enable project success.

If changes are significant in a project, the leadership role becomes more significant as compared to a complex project where the project manager's emphasis will be on planning and controlling (Anantatmula 2008). In both these scenarios, motivating team members by delegation is critical. Often, people are motivated when they are challenged and when opportunities are present to advance their career goals. There is an inherent desire among all to accomplish personal and professional goals. So, project managers must understand the personal aspirations of the project team members and support them by aligning their personal aspirations with the project goals (Anantatmula 2010). As such, it is desirable to align interests of both the individuals and the organization (Bass 1999), and such an alignment in projects, aligning individual aspirations with project goals, would pave the way for delegation of tasks and associated responsibilities among the project team members. Undoubtedly, delegation is more critical in managing agile projects.

Leadership and management styles of the project manager are not only different for plan-driven (traditional) and change-driven (agile) but also during different phases of project execution. Also, a leader's ability to communicate effectively plays a critical role in project team development, conflict management, negotiations, decision making, and project performance in both agile and traditional projects. Likewise, servant leadership is useful in managing all project teams and is readily applicable for agile projects. Servant leadership style is about delegating responsibility and encouraging participation in leadership and decision making. Delegation often helps improvements in quality, decisions, commitment, job enrichment, and better time management for leaders. It is claimed that the degree to which a leader delegates is considered as a measure of success (Sanders 2017).

A project manager is expected to direct the team, and it is a norm for traditional or plan-driven projects. However, agile project teams are expected to be self-managed. Often, agile teams comprise of people from different nationalities, cultures, languages, and values. Then, the question that comes to mind is about the appropriate leadership style of an agile project team that is global representing diversity in culture and language and values. Understanding these differences such as culture, work ethics, values, working style, and adapting to different leadership styles for different groups within the agile team while bringing all of them to common goal is the challenge often faced by agile team leaders. It is here that a leader's communication plays a key role. We will discuss communications in Chapter 5.

Team Development and Motivation

It is usual that agile project teams are comprised of people from different generations and often present challenges to team cohesion, communication, and collaboration. We often find four generations working together in project teams. People from each generation bring different attitudes, values, and work ethics to the workplace, as they are from different social and technological contexts (Anantatmula and Shrivastav 2012). Further, team relations and synergy would depend on a project's attributes such as complexity, uncertainty, unknowns, scope clarity, geographical location of team members, and external factors. As such, project teams are often involved in creative work through innovative processes. Many factors such as role definition, delegation, conflict management, and change orientation influence the team development process and influence the performance of a traditional or an agile project team. Together, these factors determine the team's collaboration and synergy that, in turn, would impact the project success such as meeting project scope, completing within budget, and meeting client requirements.

Characteristics of a project such as the type, size, unique attributes, and familiarity with the domain-specific knowledge influence project team composition and characteristics (Anantatmula 2016). It is relevant to note that striking differences exist in a project team's role and its approach to managing traditional and agile projects as fundamental differences in project characteristics exist between these two types of projects (Rogers and Anantatmula 2018). Traditional projects are managed by teams using a well-defined and comprehensive project plan. Project outcomes are clearly defined and achieved. Whereas, agile projects are faced with greater uncertainty, as scope cannot be defined completely at the outset. Consequently, agile project teams adapt a change-driven approach with incremental plans based on project progress and outcomes of the project. Agile projects are focused on increasing value and benefits to the client. Team development approaches differ for traditional and agile projects.

More importantly, the conventional *team development stage model proposed by Tuckman* (1965)—a gradual and sequential process of moving from forming to storming, norming, and finally, performing stage of team development—does not work in its pure form during the current global economy of free market philosophy, as teams will have to perform at a high level as quickly as possible to stay ahead of the competition. Further, team development cannot be viewed as a sequential and linear process. To complicate matters further, project teams are different for different projects, and a simple model may not work for all projects. For example, mega projects tend to have much larger project teams and face several issues and constraints with respect to coordination and logistics such as increased number of communication channels, more disciplines and functions, and coordination among greater number of individuals. Using Tuckman's model for team development would be very difficult in such projects. Similarly, agile projects must perform at high level right from day one, and a linear and gradual team development is not appropriate. Although individuals are assigned a specific role in the team for traditional projects, it may not be the case for agile projects. Thus, the traditional team development process of forming, storming, norming, and performing may not work as teams are required to perform right from the inception of the project.

Project teams go through various phases of development, and transitioning from one phase to the other and time spent during each phase would also depend on factors such as the organizational work culture, familiarity of the project, and behavioral issues (Anantatmula 2016). Further, the urgency (project deadlines), complexity, unknowns, risks, and costs associated with the project also influence the team development phases, duration, and transition from one phase to the other. This transition need not always be linear. All these issues and the agile approach suggest that Tuckman's model of team development may not work for agile projects.

In addition to the demands of an agile project, sometimes they are managed by multiple teams working in different nations. Geographically dispersed teams within an organization or in partnership with external organizations are often the teams that manage global agile projects. Commonly, these project teams comprise of members representing multiple organizations that cross national and international boundaries and time zones. These teams comprise of members from multiple work cultures, languages, and ethics. These complications further support our assertion that Tuckman's stage model of team development falls short because all these issues were not prevalent in 1960s and were not considered when this model was developed. Considering all these issues and challenges, a model is proposed for agile (Figure 4.1). This four-stage team development model adapts Tuckman's model and depicts sequential progress of the team from creation to achievement stage.

In the *Creation* stage, the team is put together. Team members are chosen, but processes and roles are not defined. Therefore, process- and people-related conflicts are likely to be present. Obviously, team cohesion is absent, and communication is sporadic and may not be effective.

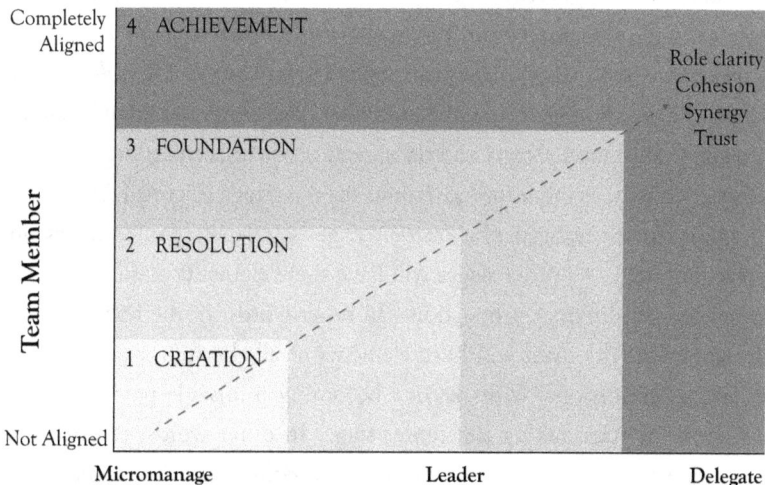

Figure 4.1 Modified Tuckman team stage development model

Transition into the *Resolution* stage is set by defining processes and making them clear to all the team members. In this stage, roles are defined, and based on the qualifications and experiences, the right person is chosen for each job. As roles are not completely clear, people-related conflicts still exist. Lack of clarity also makes it difficult to implement participative decision making. Further, team charter is developed wherein rules, team norms, behavioral expectations, responsibilities, accountability, communication, and reporting protocols are defined. The team charter, in other words, promotes team development.

In the *Foundation* stage, team processes are defined and communicated clearly with an effective communication in place, coordination, collaboration, and harmony among the team members to improve productivity. Team charter guidelines are adhered, to and conflicts are minimized. At this stage, team members participate and recommend decisions to the leader.

Once the team reaches the *Achievement* stage, team members—because of role clarity and a big picture of interdependency of tasks—understand each other's role, and individual contribution to the project becomes clear. This leads to greater cooperation and coordination among team members, and team cohesion is in place. Trust among team members is established, and participative decision making becomes the norm. Team is in high-performance mode.

All the four stages remain integral to the final stage, *Achievement*. Then, how does the transition from one stage to the other happen? And, how important is each stage as the team marches forward to the *Achievement* stage? The model suggests that the preceding stage of development becomes integral to the current stage, and time spent on the preceding stage reduces proportionately, as the team moves into the next stage (Figure 4.2).

As it can be noticed, the *creation* stage is independent, as it has no preceding stage. All other stages will have some elements of all preceding stages, but in different proportions. In other words, in the final stage of development, the team will have elements of all the four stages, but in differing proportions, with *creation* becoming miniscule part of it and achievement stage taking the center stage. In other words, roles of the preceding stage gradually reduce in the succeeding stage, but some functions of each stage work in the final *Achievement* stage. By the time a team

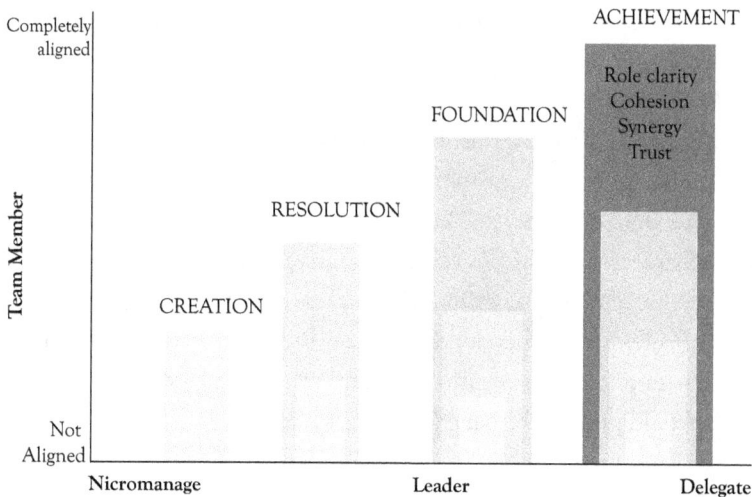

Figure 4.2 Team transition from stage to stage

reaches the *Achievement* stage, trust is fully established among the team members because of all the actions taken during the foundation stage, including the team charter. You can recognize that the team has established trust when you notice that team members demonstrate the trust by their actions such as:

- Embrace accountability
- Do not tolerate violations of the trust
- Encourage failing forward promptly
- Provide psychological safety to all in the team members
- Take initiative and exhibit self-starting behavior
- Engage in open and honest communication
- Show respect
- Develop relations
- Strive for transparency

All these actions confirm that the team is self-managed and motivated to perform at a high level and aim for excellence.

It must be noted that the proposed team development model (Figures 4.1 and 4.2) is not significantly different from Tuckman's *forming-storming-norming-performing* model. The fundamental difference between these models is that stages are not exactly sequential and overlap each other in the proposed model.

Agile prefers to have long-standing product teams instead of short-standing project teams. By using the same team at least twice and often repeatedly, much of the team development occurs already, and it promotes both efficiency and effectiveness. Long-standing product teams also make sense, as agile projects tend to develop solutions incrementally and provide one value at a time. Under these circumstances, prior understanding of what was developed and how the new solution will be integrated with prior work essential. For these reasons, long-standing product teams would prove to be beneficial.

Decision Making

Delegation of authority, responsibility, and accountability are indicators of the power distance culture in an organization. It is not unusual to find that project teams play a role in participative or group decision making when the project team matures and transition into the final stage of achieving project goals.

Prior to this progression, three scenarios of decision making emerge for the creation, resolution, foundation, and achievement stages of the team development. During the creation stage of the project team and subsequent resolution stage where differences are addressed, the senior manager or leader makes the decision. In the foundation stage where rules and processes are established, project team members participate in discussions and leave it to the manager to make a final decision. During the final phase of achieving the project goals, the decision is made by consensus as the project leader and team members participate. Transition to the final stage in the shortest time possible is critical for agile project teams, as the preference in agile is to encourage and enable team members to collectively make as many decisions as possible. People who set their own direction are often more motivated to both prove their decision was good and to do so quickly (Table 4.2).

"Delegation and decision-making style, to some extent, lets you know the power distance situation and to what extent teams are self-managed. With the increased diversity in workplaces and an opportunity to work

Table 4.2 Decision making and leadership during various stages of team development

Team	Characteristics	Team member's position	Leadership approach
Creation	• Process- and people-related conflict exist • Role clarity is absent • Team cohesion is absent • Communication is not effective	• Focus on self • Not aligned with the team • Not aware of the team's goals • Wait until you are given instructions • Problem is deferred to the leader	• Manage issues closely • Provide direction • Understand team members • Make decisions • Tell what is expected from team members
Resolution	• Process become clear • Selection of right person for right job • Role clarity is partly clear • People-related conflicts exist • Team cohesion is absent • Participative decision-making is absent	• Roles are clear • Still in the process of aligning with team • Unclear interdependency of tasks • Unclear interdependency of people • Communication process is not confirmed • Ask the leader what to do • Decisions are taken by the leader	• Provide direction • Control conflicts • Eliminate negative emotion • Define roles • Facilitate team interaction • Encourage team members to participate • Gather information and make decisions
Foundation	• Team processes are defined • Communication channels are established • Team rules and norms are defined • Team charter is developed • Importance of coordination is realized • Individuals recommend decisions	• Clear roles and responsibilities in team • Clear about performance expectations • Team processes are understood • Conflict resolution process is clear • Decisions are deferred to the leader • Recommend and then take action	• Establish processes • Communicate expectations • Provide and receive feedback • Transparent in communication • Facilitate meaningful interaction • Support team members for their initiative
Achievement	• Team members understand each other • Individual contribution to project goal clear • Cooperation and coordination among team • Team cohesion is achieved • Trust among team members is established • Participative decision-making is the norm	• Require minimum supervision • Initiate change management process • Manage risks by coordinating with team • Take responsibility • Manage self and help others in the team • Act and then inform the leader	• Support team in managing risk • Establish group decision-making process • Facilitate cooperation • Develop synergy • Encourage participative decision making • Delegate responsibility with accountability

with people from different cultures and countries in workplace, one needs to be aware of team members' expectations of the one's role and leadership style as the project manager. People from different cultures use different logical approaches such as inductive and deductive reasons for making decisions. Flexibility and adaptability of leadership and management styles are important to one's success in leading diverse project teams and global projects" (Anantatmula 2016, pp. 76–77). This is apt for agile projects.

In an investigation of extreme teams—comprising of highly skilled members who are required to collaborate in managing urgent, unpredictable, interdependent, and highly consequential tasks while simultaneously coping with frequent changes in team composition and training their teams' novice members—such as medical teams, preferred shared leadership of dynamic delegation (Klein, Ziegert, Knight and Xiao 2006). This description of *extreme teams* can be easily identified with agile project teams. In such teams, dynamic delegation and passing on leadership and decision making to team members are necessary. And, they are certainly applicable for agile project teams, which encounter frequent changes and uncertainties often.

Team Roles

In the end, each team member is responsible for promoting team harmony. Team members benefit one and all by:

- Promoting team harmony through knowledge sharing
- Communicating frequently and openly
- Participating in decision-making and supporting decisions
- Providing feedback to each other to promote engagement
- Seeking help and offering help
- Committing to the team goals unconditionally
- Striving for excellence in project execution

There are several team roles for agile project teams, as shown in Table 4.3. We first cover the three primary roles that are normally included. Then, we cover additional roles that are sometimes used. In small

Table 4.3 Agile team roles

Primary Roles	Supporting Roles
• Team Member • Scrum Master (Facilitator) • Product Owner	• Sponsor • Agile Coach • Stakeholder • Subject Matter Expert (SME)

organizations especially, one person may hold more than one role. In larger, more complex organizations, more of the additional roles are seen. Titles for many of these roles vary.

Primary Agile Team Roles

- *Team member* is a person who works on a project in cooperation with others to develop the solution for the stakeholder. Team members perform all technical and other related functions that are necessary to develop the solution. They identify the problem and develop a solution. Team members jointly plan, make decisions, hold each other accountable, and share openly with each other. Typical agile teams often include 5 to 9 team members, but some are larger or smaller.
- *Scrum master* is the one who facilitates and guides the team to improve performance, removing roadblocks so that the members can focus on their work. This role is sometimes called facilitator in forms of agile that are not scrum or part scrum. Scrum masters sometimes also participate in developing the solution. The scrum master is the servant leader to the team, helping to keep impediments out of the way of team members. Scrum masters care deeply about both the development of their team members and the usefulness of the products they are creating.
- *Product owner* is the person who represents the client or customer and other stakeholders, prioritizing work and making timely decisions enabling an agile project team. A product owner communicates the needs and interests of the external stakeholders to the development team and the team's ability

and status to the stakeholders. So, she or he is in a position to clarify or verify the solution, and if answers are not clear, it is the responsibility of the product owner to find out from the client and communicate back to the project teams. Product owners also communicate from the team to the myriad of stakeholders. Product owners also prioritize the agile team-work and verify that completed work meets the agreed-upon definition of done.

All three of these roles (team member, scrum master and product owner) perform some of the duties a project manager would on a traditional project, but often, some of the decision making that the product owner performs would typically be done by the sponsor on a traditional project. Note that while agile projects still are planned and managed, there is no one person designated as a project manager.

Additional Agile Team Roles

- *Agile coach* is someone who guides team members in learning to work more effectively by collaborating with each other and who promotes agile in the broader organization. The coach also often takes an active role in promoting agile within the broader organization, helping various stakeholders understand what they can do to help the agile teams and what they should avoid that may hinder the agile teams. An agile coach is also known as team coach, enterprise coach, and specialized coach.
- *A stakeholder* is someone affected by the project such as an end-user, indirect user, or manager. Stakeholders can hold many positions. Stakeholder as an end-user will use the solution. Stakeholder as a principal, is the decision maker who pays and implements the solution. Stakeholders as partners to the project team will help solution work in the production and integrate with the existing systems. Stakeholders as insiders are the members of the development team and provide services to the team.

- *A sponsor* is the person who wants the project to be completed, provides resources, often controls the budget, represents top management, and makes major decisions. The sponsor communicates to the project team and to top management and other key stakeholders. Many times, there is not a sponsor, and these duties are handled by the product owner. If both roles exist, they should communicate often with each other.

- *Subject matter expert (SME)* is an authority regarding a subject or discipline such as technology, process, business, or any other aspect that is of importance to the project. This person leads discussions in a facilitating manner to the extent possible, but retains ultimate authority for making technical decisions. On some projects, different team members informally assume the role of SME and strive to get the team to make decisions by consensus. On other agile projects, the scrum master serves as the SME. On larger agile projects, often, one person is good at motivating team members and removing impediments for them, and that person serves as a scrum master, while another person has the best technical knowledge and skill, and that person serves as the SME or the technical leader.

In traditional projects, team members can assume different roles such as a leader, planner, communicator, scheduler, executioner, or coordinator. These roles are assigned based on the strengths of the individual. On the contrary, agile team members decide among themselves who will perform each work activity—this is the essence of emergent leadership. However, certain other team functions such as working together, participating in decision making, and resolving conflicts are similar for both traditional and agile teams. It is worth mentioning that the team communication process is quite different in agile teams, and it is discussed in Chapter 5.

Leadership on agile projects is conducted in a different fashion. First, multiple roles each have some leadership responsibility, including team members themselves. And, second, the styles of effective agile leadership include transformational, servant, and emergent leadership. As team members have a more engaged role and are ideally together for long periods of time, their development and motivation are of primary concern. Decision making is dispersed. While different agile approaches use different titles and slightly different suggestions of responsibilities, we emphasize the three primary roles of team member, scrum master, and product owner. We briefly discuss four additional roles that sometimes are used. The last point to consider for those who know traditional project management is that all of the responsibilities of a project manager are still performed, but by multiple roles.

Summary

The agile method prefers servant and emergent leadership approaches that are different from the traditional approach of top-down leadership of command and control. Servant and emergent leadership assume significance as team member active participation in planning and innovating is required to develop solutions and increase value to the customer. In this chapter, we present concepts such as servant leadership, emergent leadership, self-managed teams, respect for all team members, selection of motivated people, creating avenues for motivation, and participative decision making. The chapter also presents a team development model and describes team evolution at various stages of the development. Our discussion in this chapter also includes the roles and responsibilities of the scrum master, team members, product owner, and supporting roles. A disciplined self-managed team with motivated team members is critical for success in an agile environment.

Questions

1. What are the pros and cons of servant and emergent leadership for agile projects, and how are they better suited in your agile project?
2. Would you agree with the team development model proposed in the chapter? Why or why not?
3. Various team roles and responsibilities are presented in the chapter. How many of them are generally present in your agile project? Are their responsibilities different from what is described in the chapter?

CHAPTER 5

Effective Communication and Collaboration

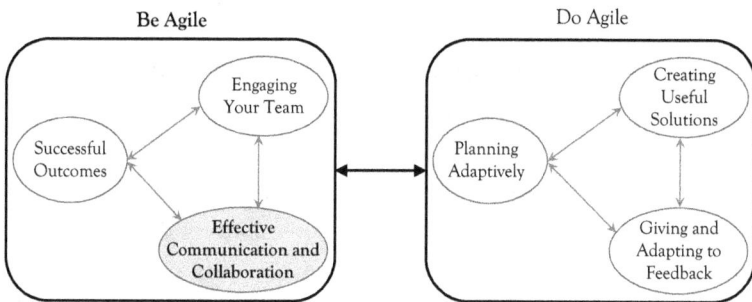

Communication in agile teams is a challenge for several reasons. Agile teams often employ face-to-face medium for communication. The pandemic is changing this scenario, and many organizations, to the extent possible, switched to virtual office and virtual meetings; many people are working remotely. As such, agile teams also use virtual medium, and a combination of face-to-face and virtual mode as well. In fact, the other two mediums are in vogue because of the nature of projects and availability of expertise. Each one of them uses different strategies for effective communication. In addition to composition of the agile team, uncertainty and risks associated with agile projects can influence communication and its effectiveness. No matter which type agile team it is, effective communication is critical for success.

After reading this chapter, you will be able to:

1. Describe the key communication challenges and which are the most effective communication methods or techniques on your project.

2. Describe transparency and tell why it is so important on agile projects.
3. Tell what constitutes timely feedback, and how does that impact your agile project.

At times, agile project teams work in a situation similar to crisis, and the absence of clear communication could prove to be a disaster. People representing diverse cultures, more so with agile project teams, present many challenges such as different perceptions of power-distance relations, M-Time versus P-Time, high-context versus low-context culture, and work ethics, which are explained later in this chapter.

Added to the cultural diversity, agile project teams may also be comprised of people from different generations such as Baby Boomers, Gen X, and Gen Y. These different generations represent different values, attitudes, and work ethics. Also, one generation may perceive another generation negatively. For example, research has shown that Gen Y people are viewed unfavorably, and they struggle to work with other generations. Understanding these differences and how to mitigate them are important.

Team Location and Communication

It is certainly true with agile project teams they comprise of members representing internal face-to-face teams, external and geographically dispersed virtual teams. It is a reality in today's business world. Specifically, many software development businesses span multiple continents, time zones, and represent different political, social, and work environments. In this global economy, organizations are increasingly compelled to establish a presence in multiple countries, and people routinely collaborate across national boundaries. The intent of virtual and geographically dispersed teams is to engage the best people with expertise, knowledge, and skills, irrespective of the location. As organizations continue to outsource activities, the reality of virtual and geographically dispersed teams presents a continuing challenge for individuals, teams, companies, and governments. With the reality of outsourcing and working with key vendors of software, project teams may be comprised of people from multiple organizations or companies with varying agendas. Collaboration among people representing different cultures and beyond geographical boundaries influence communication strategy and management.

Cultural Differences and Communication

Culture is the set of behaviors and beliefs that are characteristics of a particular social, ethnic, or age group. *Work culture* is the set of shared beliefs, values, and practices of individuals or groups in an organization, and it influences norms and behavior of both individuals and groups of that organization. In the context of managing projects, work culture of an organization influences a project team's cohesion, communication, collaboration, and conflict resolution. All these factors impact project performance.

The growth of the global marketplace and the desire to expand business into other regions and countries compel companies to use multicultural teams. Multicultural teams allow businesses to attract people based on expertise from a global perspective and to leverage their knowledge of the political, social, and work cultures and local language. However, globally distributed, multicultural teams have a tendency to fracture into subteams or subgroups that stand in conflict with one another. This would present a huge challenge to communication. Cultural differences are mainly considered in terms of P-time versus M-time and high- and low-context cultures.

P-Time and M-Time

Polychronic time (P-Time) and *monochronic time (M-Time)* are often less recognized facts of our lives. *M-Time* is focusing on one thing at a time, and it requires careful planning. Industrialized societies adapt this time scale, and they consider time to be specific and real. Time is specific and real for these nations. People, who are accustomed to M-time, allow the time to control their lives. These individuals prefer to be on time for meetings and make their best effort to complete their work on time. Industrialized nations like Germany, Japan, and the United States are good examples.

P-Time culture, on the other hand, values human interactions and relations over time and materialistic things. Work completion time is often unpredictable. Work gets done at one's own pace and is often unpredictable. People often come late for appointments. Nations with a long history and traditions who retain their values fall into this second category. Good examples are Spain, France, and Italy.

P-Time orientation is more fluid, whereas M-Time orientation is much stricter. Moreover, these two time cultures can be witnessed in different nations but not together in a single nation. When managing a team of diverse people from different cultures, you need to understand the cultural differences of M-time and P-time.

High- and Low-Context Culture

In a *high-context culture*, we must understand everything that is said in the situation that you are in. You cannot take the literary meaning of what people from the high-context culture say, and you must understand unspoken words and unwritten rules. Contextual elements help people to understand the rules. You cannot take the literary meaning of what people say. It is important to understand what is unspoken and what the unwritten rules are. Countries with a long history and traditions such as China, India, Japan, France, Germany, Spain, and France fall into this category.

Low-context culture is straightforward; what you say is what you mean. There are no hidden messages associated with what you say. Communication tends to be more direct and transparent. Relatively, it is easy to establish trust with people and businesses of a nation with a low-context culture. Countries like the United States, Canada, Australia, and the Netherlands fall into this category.

Greater dissimilarity in nationality within a multicultural team demands more direction from a team leader (Troster and Knippenberg 2012).

The research we use refers to *team lead*. For plan-driven projects, that is more commonly known as project manager. For agile projects, it is more commonly known as scrum master. When referring to findings from literature, we will use the term team lead. When referring to agile projects specifically, we will use the term scrum master.

By extension, a team lead with more dissimilarities within the project team will be required to employ more directive communication with the team members. However, a team lead's role of directing the team is an expected norm for plan-driven projects, whereas agile project teams are expected to be self-managed (Kloppenborg et al. 2018). Then, the question that comes to mind is about the appropriate leadership style of a global agile project team that comprises of cultural diversity, language, ethics, and values.

Interestingly, past research found that cultural diversity had no significant impact on communication effectiveness but agreed that cultural diversity had a negative impact on social integration. Further, research found no significant difference in the communication risks between colocated and geographically dispersed project teams, which suggests a reduced impact by technology. Even if communication may not be an issue, social integration is important for the team cohesion and collaboration, which would remain as challenges to overcome. Also, communication is still an independent variable and important for the success of a traditional and agile project. Effective communication is the only way to overcome challenges associated with ineffective social integration. Further, integrating and distributing knowledge gained from multicultural teams may help in leveraging resources and processes outside of the team, and effective communication is the means to accomplish this.

To sum up, without a proper flow of communication, all projects—traditional or agile—will fail. Specifically, communication is a necessary skill for anyone in a leadership role. Without the ability to communicate well via multiple mediums and modes, a team lead may not be successful in guiding his or her team to success. Past research has concurred this fact that communication is a critical success factor in project performance. It is essential to establish effective communication and cooperation among the team lead, stakeholders, and team members. Both traditional and agile projects use virtual and geographically dispersed teams, and team leads must go beyond the mechanical means and methods of communication to address the cultural and language differences among the team members. These challenges are often masked by the lack of face-to-face meetings and difficulties exacerbated by misunderstandings that come from the lack of skills in a common language and culture. Inability to meet face to face reduces the richness of communication among team members and increases the difficulties in leading virtual and geographically distributed project teams.

Team leads must understand and develop the flow of communication with an intent to affect the status and progress of their project positively. To meet several of the challenges aforementioned, succinct communication is necessary, and one of them is called savage summary. The term *savage summary* refers to the briefest description of an idea or tool to help people understand it. In other words, a savage summary presents an idea in a minimum number of words possible without failing to get the message across. An example of a savage summary for our next term is *Transparency*: all people openly present the facts as they are to create necessary trust.

Transparency

It is critical for product owners and scrum masters to state simple and lucid project goals and likely project outcomes during the early stages of a project. This can happen only when the project requirements are clearly defined. If these requirements are not defined well, the project may experience rework, which would lead to time and cost overruns. Agile projects typically do not have requirements defined at the start, but outcomes are a little bit more clear. Therefore, communication is the way to gradually to clarify them.

Among many benefits, transparency in communication helps teams perform better, as it improves collaboration, cohesion, cooperation, and healthy conflict. Transparent communication also contributes significantly in establishing trust among the team members and all stakeholders. Ultimately, the goal of the effective and transparent communication is to improve team and project performance.

Leadership can facilitate or constrain the free flow of information. As a team lead, it is important to address and satisfy personal and professional aspirations of team members, as it will have a strong effect on team performance. This requires a candid dialogue or transparent communication between the scrum master and team members. The other factors that would influence team and project performance are the team lead's ability to resolve conflict, develop mutual trust and respect, and establish effective communication channels across organizational lines, internal and external stakeholders.

A major obstacle to project success includes poorly defined communication processes, whereas success factors are the abilities of leaders and team members to articulate and communicate problems and solutions effectively. With this in mind, it is critical to develop a communication structure plan (Figure 5.1). This high-level plan is different from the stakeholder management plan of a traditional project management in terms of formality, frequency, medium, and the responsible party of the communication.

Figure 5.1 is shown for illustration purpose and this is often employed for informally planning communication. Most of the communication takes place face to face or through video conferencing. A plan and common understanding are necessary for effective communication. Figure 5.1 suggests that the formal communication plan in a document format is not encouraged. Consequently, different tools and techniques are considered in agile project teams for communication purpose.

It is not always necessary that communication takes place from the project team to the client as the client or the representative of the client remains a member of the project team and interacts with the team informally on a daily basis. Both informal and formal communication processes are used routinely, with a greater emphasis on informal and face-to-face communication. Many conflicts among the team members often are the result of absence of transparency and consequent misunderstanding.

Stakeholder	Item	Frequency	Owner	Importance	Medium	Comments
Client	Status Update	Daily	Project Lead	High	Face-to-Face	Business Value
Stakeholder						
Coach						
Product Owner						

Figure 5.1 *Communication management plan*

Furthermore, tools such as *Kanban boards* and *daily scrums* (aka stand-up meetings), help transparency.

Kanban board: Visible information register that communicates work status as to do, in progress, or done.

Daily scrum (aka standup): Brief meeting where member shares what done, what planned, and problems.

Conflicts can also exist with internal and external stakeholders. Both technical and people-related conflicts occur in agile. This is where transparency in communication is of immense help in resolving conflicts as increasing levels of trust, open and candid communication among the project team members and stakeholders, and good active listening skills prove to be useful in conflict resolution. Those who lead agile teams must encourage open communication, instill high levels of trust, and establish a safe environment for information exchange.

In essence, by communicating with transparency, team leads can establish an environment of openness and trust. As a result, team members establish practices for communicating project goals, expectations, and likely project outcomes. Together, all these actions instill trust among the project team and the leader. You must note that establishing trust usually takes time, but projects are time-bound, thereby challenging the team lead to overcome it. One of the ways to overcome this problem is to keep the team together once trust among the team members is established. Trust encourages project team members to collaborate, network, and innovate. Open communication and trust will lead to sharing experiences and knowledge, and together, they promote team's effectiveness and productivity.

Feedback and Timeliness

Timely feedback is essential as clients' requirements change frequently and teams often work in a highly complex work environment. Agile teaches us how to deliver in this fast-changing environment. Feedback assumes greater importance, as agile embraces this concept of change and ability to change. The agile manifesto requires client or customer collaboration all the time, and timeliness is ensured to some extent for this reason.

As such, the agile approach is to question everything and let everyone contemplate why something is the way it is. People should be comfortable and face these questions with an open mind. The team lead or coach must emphasize the following aspects during team interactions, with specific reference in the context of providing feedback to each other:

- Focus on the issue and not on the person whose idea it will be
- Accept feedback based on merit and not on person providing the feedback
- Set aside personal opinion and ego
- Be defenseless when personal errors are discovered
- Adopt self-sacrifice attitude
- Contribute actively to problem-solving meetings
- Develop an approach of continual availability
- Support participation and open conversation
- Emphasize on acceptance criteria in decisions
- Assume positive intent

As timeliness is everything in a fast-paced agile project, teams have a meeting every day for 15 minutes, which is known as a *daily scrum* (aka standup). When virtual teams dispersed geographically are employed, a mutual meeting time is set up that is optimally convenient for all. As time is of the essence, the team agenda focuses on the following issues only:

- What you did yesterday
- What is your plan today?
- Any impediments (risk or technical issue)
- Risks are identified

When an impediment or risk is a concern and may affect the team's commitment to the sprint progress, the scrum master along with technical experts continue the meeting with the responsible team member briefly to resolve the issue. However, it is a norm that other members may stay after the meeting to tackle the issues. Remember the entire team committed to the sprint goal, so they have the option of staying in the conversation. E-mails are not used for communication. By default, only face-to-face communication and discussions are used to the extent practical.

The Learning Process

This approach is very similar to what is recommended in the knowledge management literature. The team lead plays an important role in creating and nurturing a learning environment for capturing, analyzing, storing, disseminating, and reusing lessons learned from projects. Lessons learned should include both success and failure stories, which is not possible without establishing trust among the project team members. As shown Figure 5.2, the team lead and project team would seek support from each other and peers in the organization *before the project is started* in order to learn the likely challenges of the project such as complexity, uncertainty, and unknowns associated with similar projects.

While planning and executing the project, the scrum master and the team would, on a daily basis, address the following questions at the end of each working day:

- What was supposed to happen?
- What actually happened?
- What is the reason for the deviation?
- What can be done about it?

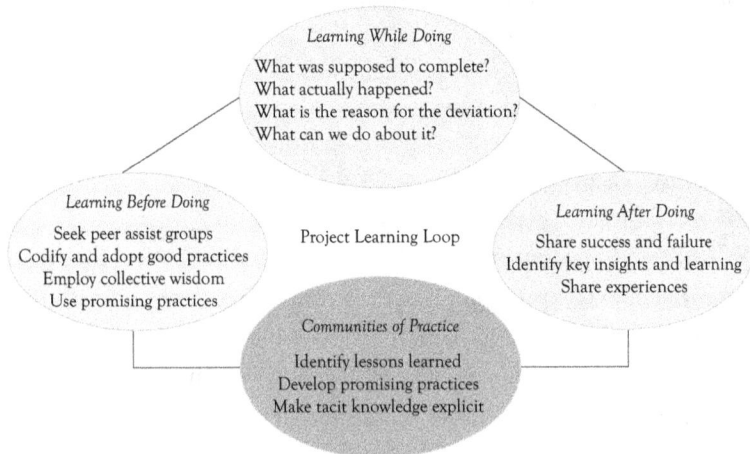

Figure 5.2 Team learning process

Adopted from: Anantatmula (2016). Project Teams.

This approach helps the project team to recognize early warning signals and take timely corrective actions, thereby preventing cost and time overruns. "Learning while doing" should not be time-consuming as these questions are addressed on a daily basis. Meetings to address these questions should be short with a clear agenda. Learning after completing the project remains an important step in this process, as the team lead and the team will have the benefit of a complete and comprehensive understanding of what went wrong and what went right. However, this practice, although desirable, is not popular and not practiced.

Feedback becomes a bit more complicated when project teams work with contractors and virtual teams. Video conferencing is a possible solution, but it has limitations as compared with face-to-face communication. In such cases, communication gap and effective feedback are the challenges that team will have to deal with. Team building exercises and developing a deeper understanding of working styles of all entities would help to some extent.

Routine feedback on work and daily interactions with the team improved bonding and team spirit among the team members. Problems and conflicts can be resolved sooner. It is obvious that project team members should take feedback in right perspective, and team members cannot be defensive of their actions. They should also be receptive and open to suggestions.

Collaboration

Often, agile project teams will have to perform in exigency mode. Cohesion and teamwork are essential from the moment the team starts working on the project. For better collaboration and to eliminate communication gap, a businessperson known as the product owner sits with the colocated team throughout the project. The collaboration in an agile team is directed at supporting each other, with a goal to provide business value to the customer. Several collaborating tools are employed for this purpose.

Daily Progress Board or Scrum Board

This board is both a communication and a collaboration tool. You may find a wide range of formats for this tool, but in general, the board is

Story	Not Started	In Progress	Completed	Testing

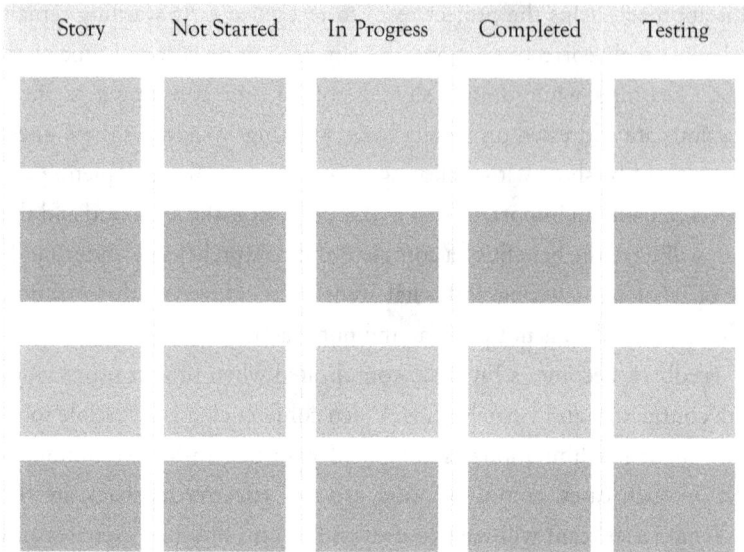

Figure 5.3 Daily progress (Scrum) board

divided into four parts, as shown in Figure 5.3. This tool is commonly used in agile projects to monitor daily work progress.

It also serves as a good communication tool to present project activity status with all the team members and key stakeholders. People working on the project post their stick notes in different columns depending on the category it belongs to, and stories flow from left to right in this board. You may find many variations to this tool and different practices in different organizations. However, the main purpose is to let everyone concerned know the status of project activity (story), current progress (work in progress, completed, or not yet started). This information is updated continuously and throughout the project execution.

A daily progress board will help avoid unnecessary progress monitoring meetings and will guide team action if the project is not progressing as per the daily plan. In addition to daily activity status, predecessor–successor relations among these activities can be drawn by using threads linking activities either using the daily progress board or creating a separate board similar to the scrum board. To sum up, this is an effective tool for project status and collaboration. Tools such as scrum board compel agile team members to denote responsibility of activities. It will also encourage team members to share ownership of all team products, as one can visualize the interdependency of all project activities. Sharing ownership promotes making statements that begin with *we* instead of one person's name. Additionally, this tool helps to build trust and open exposure of self (transparency). Finally, weekly meetings and lunches can be planned to improve bonding and collaboration.

Organizational Issues

Organization structure and culture influence agile project teams, as they are integral to the organization and share values and philosophy. On its part, an organization must be agile and believe in agile manifesto principles and adapt them in daily routine. Having project team members from multiple companies adds significant complexities to the organization structure. These could include outsourced resources, commercial vendor staff people, and expert consultants.

The organizational discipline to complete projects within the timeframe is critical as agile projects are often time-constrained. Likewise, teamwork, collaboration, effective communication, and servant leadership are some of the systems the organization must develop to "being agile and then doing agile." All these organizational issues will provide favorable results only when the right people are employed. It is very important to hire people not for technical skills but for their attitudes. People can be trained for technical skills, but it is relatively difficult to change their attitude. Additionally, people should be self-motivated to excel in their work without supervision.

Apart from the core values such as teamwork, collaboration, and transparency in communication, and organizational culture of managing agile projects can be evident from their effort eliciting project requirements accurately. The suggested approach involves an exercise for each element to capture requirements and to calculate associate time estimate, which is called planning poker, where the product owner sits in the middle with all relevant squad members on the round table. All people responsible for the work element will be involved and will be asked to estimate the time to complete the work and effort required. Extreme numbers (lowest and highest) are eliminated (like Olympics Gymnastics scoring), or they are questioned about the content of the work and risks they considered in determining the duration; everyone participates in the discussion. This round-table process continues till the entire team agrees to duration and effort (this would help in determining the cost and schedule of a project as well as risks are being identified and rectified or built in into the schedule and cost).

Scaling

Usually, agile project teams comprise of small teams. However, often an enterprise attempts to implement agile practices to meet enterprisewide demands and large projects. The principle of scaling is to increase the number of teams and frameworks while keeping the individual team size the same. Scaled agile approach generally employs a *scrum of scrums*, a concept wherein each team is represented in a meeting of all teams. This higher level meets a few times every week to develop higher-level planning and to resolve common impediments. The scrum of scrums can scale further, if required. In this situation, a project team comprising of several teams, effective communication is a major challenge.

For scaling agile to be successful, five tips are suggested. They are:

1. Employ consistent processes and practices
2. Acquire support and sponsorship from the executive leadership
3. Employ common tools
4. Use agile coaches
5. Provide an internal agile support team

It is apparent that employing consistent processes and tools and employing common tools would help effective communication immensely. Agile coaches and an internal agile support team indirectly help communication by providing additional layers of collaboration and consistency in executing projects.

Scaled Agile Framework (SAFe) is an enterprise-level framework that facilitates planning at various levels such as team, program, and portfolio. Shared resources, consistency in team processes, and integration at the portfolio level help in developing a consistent communication process for the entire enterprise.

In *Disciplined Agile Delivery (DAD)*, the emphasis is placed on people and their roles over processes in scaling agile. The primary team roles—such as team lead, product owner, team member, architecture owner, and stakeholder—are present in every team, irrespective of its size. Consistency in roles and team members also promote consistency and clarity in communications management.

Summary

In a project situation of uncertainties, and absence of complete understanding of desired outcomes of the project, effective communication is critical. Face-to-face meetings facilitate transparency in communication and possible frequent interactions with the client to provide and receive timely feedback, which are critical constituents of effective communication. However, face-to-face meetings are not always possible in every situation, and use of technological tools can be employed to improve effective communication. Team members need to collaborate effectively with each other and with various stakeholders. Transparency, timely feedback, and collaboration are critical to improve communication. A few organizational issues must also be addressed to enhance communication effectiveness.

Questions

1. What are the key communication challenges, and which are the most effective communication methods or techniques in your project?
2. Describe transparency, and tell why it is so important on agile projects.
3. What constitutes timely feedback, and how does that impact your agile project?

PART II

Doing Agile

CHAPTER 6

Agile Methods (Doing Agile)

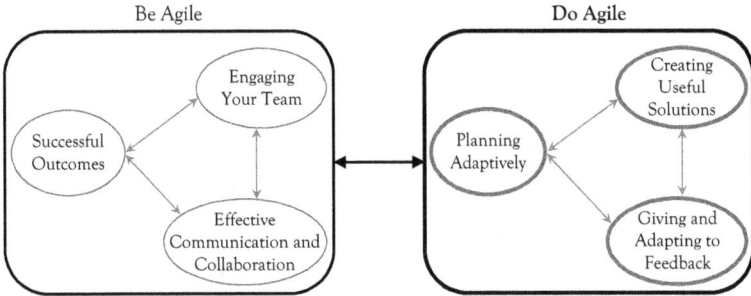

The first half of this book dealt with *being agile*, that is what understanding, believing, and acting is necessary to create a fertile ground for implementing agile. While it is impossible to state what percentage of possible improvement comes from the mindset of agile versus the actions of *doing agile*, we suspect a majority of the potential improvement, perhaps as much as two-third, comes from being agile and as little as one-third from doing agile. In other words, going through the motions without understanding and believing why you are doing so will yield far less benefit that both being and doing agile will. On the other hand, having the mindset without the tools may mean well-intentioned people are still less effective than they could be. There is much benefit to the mechanics of performing agile, and so, we describe these now. After reviewing this chapter, you will be able to:

1. Understand principles and guidelines of implementing agile
2. Deploy agile manifesto principles using tools and methods
3. Learn about tools and techniques from various agile approaches such as scrum, XP, lean/Kanban, PMI-ACP, SAFe, and Disciplined Agile

This chapter introduces some of the main tools emphasized in each agile approach. In that sense, it is similar to how Chapter 2 summarized the concepts of being agile. One key difference is that the Agile Manifesto dealt with being agile and not doing agile, so we do not report anything from the Manifesto here. We start with scrum, as that is the most prevalent method in use. We then include tools other approaches use that either to add or emphasize in a different style. Within each method, we organize the tools by topic. Table 6.1 briefly shows a few of the major types of tools that come from each of the agile approaches.

In Chapter 5 on communication, we defined an agile term—savage summaries. That is, what is the briefest few words that can be used to help people understand the gist of an idea? We do that now for each key tool. Many of these savage summaries are only six or eight words long—just enough to provide context. One challenge in reading these is often the definition of a tool includes mentioning another tool. It is impossible to define everything at the outset, so sometimes, if a tool is mentioned in a definition, it will, in turn, be defined shortly. In the remaining chapters, we describe how a number of the more frequently used tools are used and illustrate many of them with examples.

Scrum Practices

Scrum is by far the most commonly used agile approach. Scrum is prescriptive—encouraging adherents to perform in exact manners as they prioritize and perform work and seek and react to feedback. Not only is it used in its pure form frequently, it is often combined with another

Table 6.1 Sources of agile tools

• Scrum	• Lean
• Sprints, ceremonies, product, build	• Eliminate waste, flow, pull production, visual management
• XP	• PMI-ACP and Practice Guide
• Planning, test, quality	• Initial planning, continual planning, monitoring and controlling, Agile contracts
• SAFe	• Disciplined Agile
• Systems thinking	• Life cycles, governance

agile approach or with traditional project management in various hybrid approaches. Key ideas in scrum methods can be grouped into sprints, ceremonies, products, and build.

Sprints

One key aspect of scrum is all work is done in defined time buckets called sprints. These are often two- or three-week endeavors—never more than one month, but shorter durations are also in common use. The product owner prioritizes the work that is most wanted to be done first and the team decides how much they can do during the sprint and commit to it. During the sprint, few if any changes are allowed and great effort is expended, especially by the scrum master, to allow the development team members to concentrate on their work. Two or more sprints that collectively produce functionality complete enough to transition to users is called a release. In many forward-thinking companies, each release must demonstrate measurable business benefits.

Sprint (aka: increment)	Short period when committed to deliverables are created
Emergent design	Gradual understanding of the shape of a deliverable
Timebox	Defined start and stop times for agreed amount of work to be performed
Commit to work	Team promises how much they will accomplish in timebox
Planning poker (games)	Method for team to quickly relatively size-specific stories
Story point	Estimate by team of complexity and size of specific work in story form
Release	Period when functionality is created and transitioned to users

Events

Another key idea in scrum is meetings is called events or ceremonies, and there are specific suggestions (often clear directions) on how and when to have these ceremonies. A pattern to these team ceremonies is tied to each scrum team as they work through each release and sprint. While the last five are described specifically in scrum, we include all of them here for ease of understanding.

Visioning	Meeting at inception to gain agreement on expected outcomes
Release planning	Scope current release and envision high-level view of future
Product backlog refining	Understand, slice, and estimate time to create user stories
Sprint planning	Select stories from backlog, plan and commit to sprint
Daily scrum (aka standup)	Each member shares what is done, what is planned, and problems
Sprint review or demo	Team demonstrates product, and product owner determines if it is done, next work is identified
Retrospective	ID lessons learned, plan to improve people, process, and product

Product

The deliverables that are created are called product. Agile places great emphasis on progressively determining what product will be developed and ensuring it satisfies customers' needs.

Product	The deliverables that are created on an agile project
Product backlog	A wish-list of things that may be created by the project team
Release backlog	The work that is planned to be completed in current release
Sprint backlog	The work that is committed to be completed in current sprint
Prioritized backlog	Desired products prioritized by business value and risk

Product increment	The deliverables created and accepted during a sprint
Artifacts	Backlogs and product increments
Epic	Large functionality or product, not defined enough to produce
User story	Need described by who wants it, how they will use it, and why
Slicing user stories	Breaking stories into smaller stories that can be created in days
Definition of done	Agreement on exactly how the deliverables produced will be judged

Build

Building is creating the products and services the customers want. This effort ideally makes up a large percentage of the time scrum workers spend on a project. On any project, stakeholders want to know how things are progressing, and agile is no different. There are several tools used in agile to communicate status.

Definition of ready	Agreement that team understands story enough to bring into a sprint
Pivot	Changing direction on next sprint based upon customer desires
Velocity	The forecasted number of story points a team can do in one sprint
Cadence	The rhythm of planning, performing, and evaluating each sprint
Duration	The time-boxed length of sprints such as one or two weeks
Impediments	Things that can interfere with a team member doing their work
Burn down chart	Line graph showing estimated work versus actual remaining work
Burn up chart	Line graph showing estimated work versus actual completed work

XP Methods

Extreme programming or XP is another agile methodology and widely seen as giving many good ideas for the more technical aspects of developing and testing information systems. As such, it is often combined with a more organizational approach such as scrum for planning and controlling. XP methods for this book are grouped into the categories of planning, test, and quality.

Planning

While we group them separately here, XP creates plans for performing work and testing results at the same time. All of the planning and testing ideas are aimed to ensure quality from the perspective of the user.

Small releases	Provide tested, working product often to deploy to users
Right-sized	Ensuring stories are small, understood, and testable
Metaphor	Compare vision to something easier to understand
Just-in-time planning	Describe work needed for current design at the last responsible moment
40-hour workweek	Plan to work at sustainable pace
Sustainable pace	Amount of work team can consistently produce well
Embrace change	Acceptance and eagerness to serve updated customer needs
Spikes	Short, time-boxed effort to test concept or reduce risk

Test

Verifying the quality of work and deliverables is essential in agile. Testing is planned early and conducted often to ensure that any unsatisfactory work is discovered quickly and to further ensure that everything produced works seamlessly together. As many systems can be quite complicated, ensuring all components work effectively together is critical.

Test plan	Determine how you will verify work is acceptable before coding
Unit test	Ensuring small function or classes work properly, usually automated
Integration test	Ensuring new functionality works immediately in existing system
Acceptance test	Verifying for customer entre system works correctly

Quality

XP has promoted a number of practices that help to ensure the solutions that are developed work properly. Some of these ideas come directly from XP, and others have roots in the total quality movement of a generation ago and are updated and emphasized in XP.

Lean Methods

Lean management thinking was originally developed as part of the Toyota Production System. Lean has been used and adapted in agile approach to project management just as it has been in the six sigma approach to quality. Because one of the most visible tools used in lean is the Kanban board, it is sometimes called lean/Kanban or even just Kanban. The visibility of the Kanban is part of lean, but so is eliminating waste and creating an efficient workflow by pulling work through the system instead of pushing it. Next, we explain these terms.

Eliminate Waste

When striving to produce faster, less expensive, and better solutions, anything that either slows down progress, causes mistakes, or costs extra money is not valued by the customer. Lean agile teams define the minimum amount of features a solution or portion of a solution needs and determine everything beyond that is waste. The goal is to reduce it or even completely eliminate waste when possible. By working deliberately on waste reduction, teams can little-by-little make their work processes more efficient.

Flow

Lean agile methods have a continuous workflow with highly visible information. Workers pick the next work item off a prioritized list once they finish the previous item. The continual nature of the workflow enables extremely rapid response to changing demands, a stream of new functionality to be delivered quickly, feedback to be given just as quickly, and an ability for each worker to concentrate on one thing at a time and avoid the task switching waste of multitasking.

Limit work in process (WIP)	Simplify by working continuously on work started until completion
Mange flow	Teams focus on reducing time to complete work
Make process explicit	Ensure everyone understand how a process works
Improve collaboratively	When one worker has problems, others help and learn together
Throughput	The average number of units produced in a time duration
Cycle time	The time from when work starts on an item until it is delivered

Pull Production Model

New work is not pushed into production due to a schedule or plan. Workers only start working on a new item when they finish the previous one. This is accomplished by using a Kanban board to visually communicate the work that is complete, in process, or waiting to be started and only starting a predetermined number of items until some of them are complete.

Optimize the whole	Teams look at what the whole needs, not just their needs
Build quality in	Workflow is reduced and waste increased if mistakes are made
Defer decisions	By making decisions as late as possible, teams have better information

Queue duration and length	Lean teams strive to reduce time work spends waiting
Lead time	Shorter lead time make better service and faster feedback
Bottleneck	The portion of work process that limits amount and speed

Visual Management Tools

A key tenet of lean is visual management. The primary means of doing this is Kanban boards where all work to be done, in process, and completed are displayed with cards that represent individual work items.

Kanban board	Visible information register that communicates work status
Task card	Sticky note or index card showing work item name and other info
3C process	Task card with conversations and confirmation of understanding

PMI-ACP Exam Outline and Agile Practice Guide Methods

The purpose of PMI's Agile Certified Practitioner is to recognize people who have a broad understanding of agile concepts and tools and at least a couple of years of agile experience. The purpose of the *Agile Practice Guide* is to share a common understanding of agile tools, situational guidelines, and understanding. Both of these sources are *agile agnostic*, in that they draw from various agile approaches just as we do in this book. We include tools here that are stressed in these sources but are not as visibly promoted in the other agile approaches we use in this book.

Initiating

Project initiation occurs starting when a project idea is first envisioned and ends when a project is chartered. This way of starting a project making sure everyone is on the same page is just as valid in agile projects as in any other. This includes both determining what approach or combination of approaches you will use and making sure the team members all understand and commit to the work.

Hybrid	Some hybrid approaches combine agile and plan-driven or two different agile approaches such as lean and scrum
Charter project and team	Ensure all stakeholders have a common understanding and are committed.

Initial Planning

One primary difference between agile and predictive approaches to projects is that predictive projects perform most of their planning prior to performing, while agile projects plan and perform in repeated small increments or even continually. However, there is still some planning that makes sense to perform early on agile projects. We cover that here, and in the next section, we cover planning that is more likely to occur repeatedly throughout the project life.

Product roadmap	Visual showing high-level plans of products expected to be created during each release
Refine requirements	Gain consensus on acceptance criteria
Customer prioritization	Decide importance or urgency of work based on customer input
MoSCoW	Prioritization technique of must, should, could, and will not have
Risk-adjusted backlog	To-do prioritized list of work to both create product and reduce risk
Minimal marketable feature (MMF)	A single fully functional, tested feature a customer could use
Journey maps	Simple visual showing how customers view experience
Story map	Visual with product features on top and supporting detail next

Persona	Fictional username, description, and values for solution
Value stream mapping	Visual flowchart identifying value and nonvalue activities
Premortem	Brainstorming description of what could go wrong
Risk-based spike	Short time-boxed work to address specific risk

Continual Planning

While some of the planning techniques described earlier occur primarily early in a project, the ones described here often occur repeatedly throughout the project interspersed with continued work in creating the solution.

Continuously identify risks	Specific effort to use feedback and engage team to identify risks
Refine requirements	Use feedback to progressively understand true needs
Plan at multiple levels	Project and release planning early and more detailed as needed
Share knowledge	Deliberatively capture and share tacit knowledge

Monitoring and Controlling Progress

It is essential to monitor progress on any project. Primarily people put an emphasis on openly sharing information on how a project is doing, so all team members and stakeholders can take make needed decisions and take appropriate action.

Information radiator	Highly visual display of work and supporting information
Earned value	Number of story points completed versus expected in time period
Variance analysis	Quantitative review of difference between expected and actual

Trend analysis	Quantitative review of changes in performance over time
Defect rate	Errors and bugs that have escaped from the task of creating product and may be found internally or externally
Five whys	Quality technique striving to find the root cause by asking questions

Agile Contract Types

Agile projects rely more on relationship building than on restrictive contract clauses. That said, organizations need to have contracts for purchasing supplies and services that lead to effective solutions. As there is less upfront planning, there is less opportunity to use fixed price-type contracts. Instead, there are multiple types of contracts and clauses to large contracts that promote useful sharing of risk and information on agile projects. We define a few of them here.

Fixed-price increments	Agreement to pay set amount for current increment of work
Graduated fixed price	Agreement by which a contractor makes more if completed early
Change for free	Agreement allowing customer to substitute future work packages
Money for nothing	Agreement to pay contractor portion if future work is terminated

Scaled Agile Framework (SAFe) Methods

Systems Thinking

Peter Senge considers systems thinking as a discipline of visualizing the big picture and a framework for interrelationships among various elements rather than things and for perceiving patterns of change rather than static image of it. Arnold and Wade (2015) define it as, "Systems thinking is a set of synergistic analytic skills used to improve the capability of identifying and understanding systems, predicting their behaviors, and devising modifications to them in order to produce desired effects. These skills work together as a system" (p. 675). Systems thinking can help to understand the root causes of complex behaviors within a system to better predict them and, ultimately, adjust their outcomes.

Portfolio vision	Description of desired future state of value streams and solutions
Agile release train	Ongoing team of agile teams that plans and works together
Assume variability	Preserve options to provide flexibility because of unknowns
Objective milestones	Decision points based on objective evaluation of working systems
Continuous delivery pipeline	Visual depiction of workflows and activities to produce solutions

Disciplined Agile Methods

Disciplined agile draws from many approaches to agile just as we do in this book. It offers multiple choices in how to implement agile depending on your circumstances and guidance on how to make good choices. Disciplined agile supports six different project lifecycle models and identifies 21 processes to be decided, with over 100 decision points and over 800 options with strengths and weaknesses of each option. As mentioned in Chapter 2, disciplined agile is understood by a set of principles, promises, guidelines, and beliefs that, in turn, suggest how to make the many decisions regarding lifecycle and process.

Lifecycle

Disciplined agile supports six project lifecycle models and recognizes that some teams will evolve from one to another, some will use a hybrid approach incorporating more than one model, and some teams will still use the traditional waterfall approach. We will look at the lifecycle models in the following chapter. We start with identifying the three phases that occur in lifecycle models, then the six lifecycle models, and finally, a few other related ideas. For the remainder of this book, we will use the term *initiation* for the first phase, as it is more commonly understood by many project professionals.

Inception (initiation) phase	Time from project idea until vision agreed and OK to commence (essentially the same as initiating stage in plan-driven projects)
Construction phase	Incremental planning, delivery, and feedback until release-ready
Transition phase	Readiness determined and solution released into production with support to help customer achieve desired outcomes
Agile lifecycle	Iteration-based production of solutions, including inception, construction, and transition phases
Lean (aka Kanban) lifecycle	Kanban based, visible, eliminate multitasking, reduce WIP
Program	Large development effort involving multiple coordinated teams also known as team of teams approach
Work item pool	All work to do: new requirements, defects, training, etc.
Minimum market release (MMR)	Fully functional product release with fewest acceptable features

Governance

All organizations need to monitor and encourage teams, so some oversight is needed. Disciplined agile stresses lightweight, but effective governance. The primary way this is accomplished is by utilizing the following six risk-based milestones that can be used flexibly and informally in any project lifecycle.

Stakeholder vision	Milestone at end of inception with initial scope, technology, risk, etc. are agreed
Proven architecture	Milestone early in construction when approach is verified to reduce risk
Continued viability	Milestone(s) through construction to ensure team is making progress
Sufficient functionality	Milestone late in construction when the MMR is achieved, and cost is OK to release product
Production-ready	Milestone early in transition when product is tested and complete, and users are capable to accept
Delighted stakeholders	Milestone at end of transition when product is successfully used with trained and happy users

Summary of Key Agile Tools

This chapter listed and organized over 100 of the key agile tools found in scrum, XP, lean, PMI's Exam Outline, *Agile Practice Guide*, Scaled Agile Framework (SAFe), and Disciplined Agile Manifesto. There are many more tools used by some agile teams, and any two people may have included a slightly different set in their essentials list. We gave each tool a savage summary to provide readers with a high-level idea of what it is. Now we organize all of them into a single framework, as shown in Figure 6.1, just as we did with the agile mindset ideas in Chapter 2. We organize this framework into the following three chapters:

- Chapter 7, Planning Adaptively
- Chapter 8, Creating Useful Solutions
- Chapter 9, Giving and Adapting to Feedback

Planning adaptively starts with using an agile lifecycle whether that cycle is based upon iterations, continuous flow, hybrid, or scaled. Then,

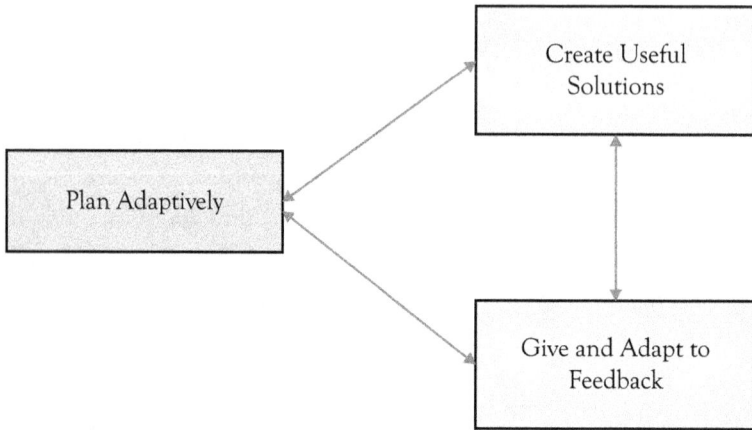

Figure 6.1 Agile tools and metrics framework

we include progressive planning, project feasibility, project initiation, and release planning.

Creating useful solutions starts with tools for product planning. It includes tools for working with backlogs, speed, flow, risks, and quality. The chapter concludes with increment planning and execution.

Giving and adapting to feedback starts with testing. It has tools for identifying problems and improving. Multiple tools for visual communication are included. It wraps up with tools for conducting effective meetings (also called events).

Summary

"Being agile" provides foundation to understanding principles and guidelines of agile. The Agile Manifesto was all about the mindset of agile, so we draw no tools or techniques from it. The same is true with other governing principles of agile. "Doing agile" deals with judicious deployment of these principles using tools and methods. We draw upon tools and techniques from each of the agile approaches mentioned so far: scrum, XP, lean/Kanban, PMI-ACP, SAFe, and Disciplined Agile. As with the mindset ideas, we attribute techniques to the agile approach that we feel make the largest contribution to each. Many of the techniques are used by more than one agile

approach. These are the techniques that translate foundational concepts of agile into actionable elements.

Questions

This chapter presented many tools and approaches. For the agile project you are currently working on:

1. Which one do you prefer to employ and why?
2. If your preferred approach and tools are different from what you are using, what are its inadequacies?

CHAPTER 7

Planning Adaptively

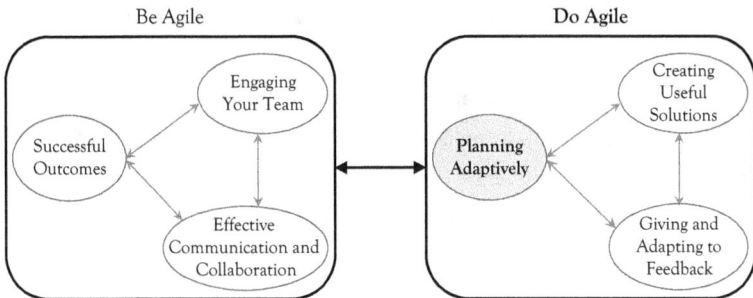

Be Agile   Do Agile

Successful Outcomes — Engaging Your Team — Effective Communication and Collaboration ⟷ Planning Adaptively — Creating Useful Solutions — Giving and Adapting to Feedback

One primary difference between traditional (plan-driven, predictive) project management and agile (change-driven, adaptive) project management is that instead of planning most of the project before most of the work is started, in agile, only enough planning is performed at the outset, so the team can get started. Altogether, agile often has at least as much planning as the traditional approach and perhaps even more. However, the planning occurs adaptively in many little sessions rather than one big one. There are multiple advantages in adaptive planning. The team can start quickly. They can show early ideas to stakeholders who can progressively decide exactly what they want. Planning is performed when enough information is at hand to make good plans. Plans can change, even radically, depending on the stakeholders without causing excessive problems to schedule or budget. In short, on many projects, adaptive planning makes great sense.

After reviewing this chapter, you will be able to:

1. Develop a clear understanding of the agile lifecycle
2. Understand various influencers of the agile lifecycle
3. Learn about agile project planning techniques
4. Define success metrics for agile projects

This chapter on planning adaptively starts with using an agile lifecycle and that cycle can be based upon iterations, continuous flow, hybrid, or scaled. Then, we include ideas and techniques regarding progressive planning, project feasibility, project initiation, and release planning.

Agile Lifecycles

The first thing to consider regarding *agile lifecycles* is how to start and end a project. There needs to be an initiation and a transition. We will describe these two, often short phases, and apply them to each lifecycle we next describe. While many agile lifecycle models are used, they tend to be variations of three primary approaches. First is the iteration-based lifecycle popularized by scrum. This lifecycle has a series of short sprints (aka iterations) with planning and commitment for what will be accomplished in each sprint. Second is a Kanban lifecycle popularized by Lean product development, in which once one work item is complete, a next item is started. The third lifecycle we will describe is hybrid. This can be a combination of the iteration-based or Kanban lifecycles and a combination of one of them with a traditional plan-driven lifecycle. The context in which a project is to be planned and performed often suggests one lifecycle model or another may be more effective.

Two more concepts are included in understanding any agile lifecycle model. First, on many agile projects, no one knows what the deliverables will look like at the project start. The gradual discovering of the deliverable and details regarding it is called *emergent architecture*. The need to discover more as a project progresses is a key aspect of agile. The other concept is *small releases*, which means the project team provides frequent, tested, working product so that the users can gain quick value and provide quick feedback.

Disciplined Agile describe three phases for projects that apply to different lifecycle models. They are *initiation*, *construction*, and *transition*. We prefer to use initiation as the name for the first phase as that is familiar with most project folks.

Initiation Phase

The initiation phase starts with the first idea about a potential project and ends when the project vision is understood and agreed upon by the key

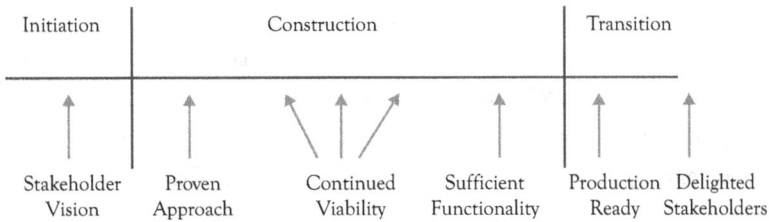

Figure 7.1 Agile lifecycle phases with governance milestones

stakeholders and the project team. XP teaches us that one way to describe a project vision is by a *metaphor*. A metaphor compares two seemingly unrelated concepts. A metaphor not only helps the team share a common vision but provides a shared vocabulary and gives the participants a story to tell about what the product of their project will become. For example, a project to create a Level 1 (the simplest) arboretum might be compared to creating a small research library. People can envision that a library contains information, and the arboretum will have information on the included trees. As it is a research library, they may need to access the information on-site or via the Internet, but may not check out materials, so signage perhaps with a phone app can be used to share information. Being small, it will not be comprehensive, and a Level 1 arboretum can contain as few as 25 species of trees, while many thousands of species exist in the world. Notice that this vision guides the project, but it still leaves a substantial amount of detail to be determined. In agile projects, that detail emerges gradually.

This milestone of sharing understanding of the project vision signifies it is OK to commence with performing the project—that is, enter the construction phase. Ideally, the majority of the time on an agile project is spent in the construction phase.

Construction Phase

The construction phase starts when the stakeholder vision is understood and agreed to and ends when the product has enough functionality that it makes sense to proceed into the transition phase. Often, one of the first things accomplished in the construction phase is to prove that the approach and technology work. This is a risk reduction strategy because if the first approach does not work, very little time is invested before deciding to use a different approach. Construction may last some time, so there are often intermediate points in which progress is assessed to make sure the project remains viable. For each of these points, the team often plans incrementally, delivers some product, and receives feedback. These intermediate points could be informal or formal. The construction phase ends when the team determines there is enough functionality that it makes sense to transition that product into production. This point is sometimes called the *minimum marketable release (MMR)*, that is, a fully functional part of a solution that is of value to the customer. Typically, there is a cost to transition, so the working functionality should have higher value than the cost of making the transition.

Transition Phase

The third and final phase is the transition phase. This phase starts by determining that both product and users are ready. The product is tested to ensure it works properly and is complete. The development team also wants to ensure users are capable of using the product. A key topic is, who will provide technical support to the module in production; it may be the agile project team, but this can cause distraction of key resources. Or, it can be a separate production support team, given they have the knowledge of the technology and the solution implemented. Once two-pronged readiness is verified, the solution is released into production. Note the name of this phase—transition. This implies that it does take some time, and rather than turning product over as a mere transaction, the team ideally works with the users in a relationship to increase the probability that the users will be successful. Near the end of transition, and frequently later also, effort is made to verify that the stakeholders are not only satisfied, but delighted.

Iteration-Based Lifecycle

The first lifecycle we discuss is the iteration-based lifecycle. It is depicted in figures 7.2 and 7.3. In Figure 7.2, you can see that there is an initiation at the start and a transition at the end. You can also see that there is one

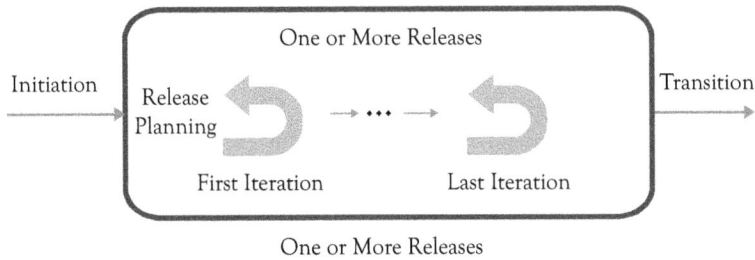

One or More Releases

Figure 7.2 Releases in iteration-based lifecycle

or more release. A *release* is when a certain amount of functionality the team has been creating is transitioned to users. It could be a complete system, a very small portion of a system, or anything in between. Each release requires planning to determine what functionality will be sent to users. Once planning is far enough along, there will be *sprints*. Often, an early iteration is designed to verify that the chosen approach will work. There may be several iterations within a release. For example, if a release is planned to take 12 weeks, perhaps iterations within it may be *time-boxed* to two weeks each, in which case, there would be six iterations within the release. Shorter projects may have only one release, but longer projects may have several.

Figure 7.3 shows more detail of what is included in each iteration. Each iteration starts with a *release backlog* of the requirements to be completed during the entire release. The team selects items from the release backlog that become *sprint backlog* of requirements to be constructed. The planning includes *prioritizing the backlog* items so that team members will know which requirement to do first. The product owner prioritizes the requirements, but the team members decide collectively how much work they can do in the upcoming iteration and then *commit* to it. This may be less work than the product owner prefers, but the team has final say based upon how much work they have done in the past. Each team member picks one item at a time from the backlog and begin work. Each day they have a brief meeting called a daily scrum (aka standup) where each team member shares what they accomplished the day before, what they plan to do this day, and any impediment that may get in their way. At the end of the iteration, the team demonstrates the product they built. The product owner, using the agreed-upon definition of done, determines if the work

Initial Planning

Build

Iteration Backlog

Daily Standups

Retrospectives

Demonstrations

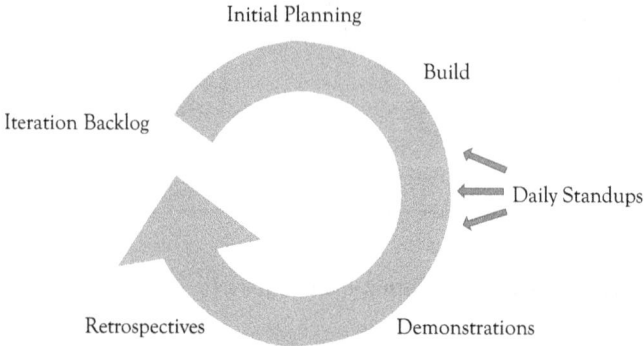

Figure 7.3 Iteration detail

is complete or not. This definition of done concept of agreeing in advance exactly how output will be judged is so helpful to team members as they perform their work. It greatly reduces stress about showing work results and increases the probability their results will be what the product owner wants. Items not completed return to the backlog for work in a future iteration. The team then holds a retrospective meeting to determine what worked well and what can be improved and makes the improvements part of the next sprint. This leads directly into planning the next iteration.

Lean Lifecycle

Figure 7.4 depicts the lean (aka Kanban) lifecycle. Note several things about it. First, it has the three phases of initiation, construction, and transition, as all lifecycle models do. One output of initiation is the set of initial requirements. The product owner prioritizes this original set of

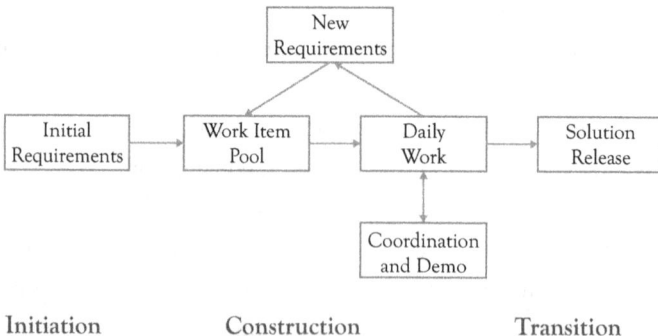

New Requirements

Initial Requirements → Work Item Pool → Daily Work → Solution Release

Coordination and Demo

Initiation   Construction   Transition

Figure 7.4 Lean lifecycle

requirements. These form the *work item pool* at the project outset. The work item pool is constantly changing. First, as team members finish one work item, they choose the next highest priority items for their daily work. Second, based upon both new suggestions from users and what team members accomplish in daily work and how the demonstrations either prove items are completed satisfactorily or not, the product owner adds, deletes, and reprioritizes items. As the product owner determines demonstrated items meet the definition of done, items are released into production. There is no set timetable for demonstrations and coordination among team members—both occur on a continual basis. That is the biggest difference between Kanban and iteration-based agile lifecycles. Product demonstrations, work coordination, and solution releases are all performed when ready—not deterministically such as once every two weeks.

Hybrid Lifecycle

The third type of lifecycle is *hybrid*. There are many variations of hybrid using at least a part of agile. Some people combine two agile approaches such as scrum and XP because scrum is good for planning and XP is good for quality. Another hybrid combination is part iteration-based where set times such as every two weeks make sense for some project deliverables, but other deliverables are welcome as soon as they are ready, and the Kanban approach makes sense. For example, work on specific features might be delivered every two weeks, while production support work might occur immediately. In both the types of these hybrid models, the two approaches may operate in parallel. Another type of hybrid lifecycle model combines agile and traditional (aka waterfall, plan-driven or predictive). In Figure 7.5, note how these may operate in series with one following another. For instance, in building a new hospital wing, perhaps the first part of the project is conducted in an iteration-based method where the architects send a rough concept to the client who has doctors, nurses, techs, and managers offer opinions. Then, the architects refine the concept based upon the feedback and send it to the client for more detailed feedback. After several rounds of increasingly detailed feedback and adjustments, a design is locked in and a detailed waterfall plan is

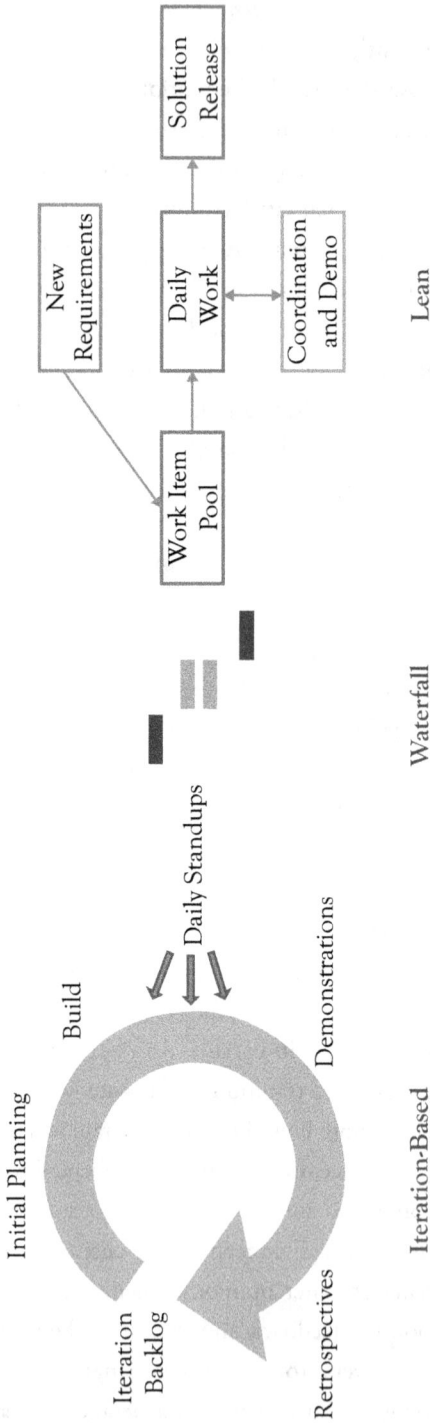

New Requirements

Solution Release

Work Item Pool

Daily Work

Coordination and Demo

Lean

Waterfall

Daily Standups

Build

Initial Planning

Iteration Backlog

Demonstrations

Retrospectives

Iteration-Based

Figure 7.5 Hybrid lifecycle example

developed. The main construction is then completed according to the detailed plan. Near the end of the project, there will certainly be a number of punch list items that need to be completed, but not necessarily in a particular order. At this point, the project could be conducted using Kanban with team members selecting one item at a time to complete when each person is ready.

Governance

One principle of agile is to do as much as needed, but no more. This is also true as organizations govern their agile projects. Any project must be governed to ensure it is making appropriate progress and to encourage and guide the development team. Savvy organizations develop methods of determining what is important to check and how informally or formally it can be done. The more informal the checks, the less stress there is all around. The most typical governance revolves around the *milestones* shown in Figure 7.1. We show some of the most commonly used tools and metrics to support the milestones in Figure 7.6. As with so many other things in agile, some of these go by slightly different names and are used in a slightly different manner depending on the agile approach used. Many of these are used primarily by the team to govern themselves. Some of the items in the early columns are either tools or leading indicators. Items in later columns tend to be results or even lagging indicators. Agile teams tend to use the tools and leading indicators to ensure they will create deliverables that will enable their clients to be successful. Note these are color coded to indicate which of the final three chapters in this book each is described.

Measured across the six governance milestones are four categories of agile project success. The first row is viability and value. The reason anyone performs a project is to provide value for stakeholders. That is, do the deliverables from the project enable the customer to achieve the outcomes they want?

The second row is predictability. Agile teams pride themselves on being able to determine how much work they can produce, and then doing what they said they would. Decision makers and clients value having confidence in knowing when deliverables will be available. Many

	Stakeholder Vision	Feasible Approach	Continued Viability	Sufficient Functionality	Production Ready	Delighted Stakeholders
Viability and Value	Team articulated vision, persona, initial backlog	MoSCoW, Prioritized backlog, Epic, User story,	MVP, MMF, Definition of Done, Reprioritized backlog, Demo	Release Decision		
Predictability	Roadmap	Journey Map, Velocity	Planning games, Cycle time, Throughput, Burndown/Burnup charts, Kanban board	MMR	Customer readiness, support readiness	
Quality		Risk spike, Premortem	Definition of ready, tests (unit, integration, and acceptance), defect rate	Escaped defects		
Happiness		Agile contract clauses	Conversatons during standups and retropectives			Customer/user Conversations and surveys

Chapter 7
Chapter 8
Chapter 9

Figure 7.6 Agile metrics and tools mapped to governance

projects have a great deal of time pressure, and predictability includes timeliness.

The third row is quality. Products must work correctly to ensure the predictability and desired value in the first two rows. Testing of all sorts is conducted as soon as possible to discover any problems and correct them quickly. One key concept in agile is to shorten the feedback cycle to make improvements immediately.

The fourth and bottom row is happiness. This is for team members and all other stakeholders. The reason for performing projects is to satisfy stakeholders. Team members perform the project work. Team members who are upset, burned out, or otherwise having problems are leading indicators of problems.

The first milestone many organizations find useful is the *stakeholder vision*. For those of you more familiar with traditional projects, this is very much like getting a *charter* drafted, discussed, improved, and agreed upon. The vision should include the goal of the project—what is the outcome our stakeholders need to be successful? While end-users, some level of management, and/or other stakeholders may have drafted this goal, the team developing the solution must buy into it and view it as attainable (even if it is aspirational). The vision often also includes the general approach and technology to be employed, the development team and their plans to work together, key risks, timeframe needed, and budgetary considerations. Ideally, this vision forms an agreement in principle and will guide the team as they work and their leadership as they govern the team. If it helps in your organizational culture, call this a stakeholder vision or a project charter.

The second typical milestone is to prove the approach selected is workable. In Disciplined Agile, this is called *proven architecture*, but we prefer to use the term feasible approach, as that is generalizable to different types of projects beyond information technology (IT). This often necessitates a short *spike* at the start of construction to test the approach. Agile teams wish to attack big risks early so that if they need to change direction, not much effort will have been wasted. This is an example of *shifting left,* which is to perform as much testing and risk reduction early to gain feedback as soon as possible so needed changes can be started quickly.

A third typical milestone may actually occur a series of times in which the team shows enough progress that leaders are convinced of the project's *continued viability*. At each of these points, a decision can be made to continue in the same direction, *pivot* to some new (and maybe altogether different) direction, or stop work. A decision to change or stop may be a good sign, in that we are cutting our losses and spending our time and effort on a new direction or perhaps an entirely new project.

The fourth typical governance point is when a team decides they have *sufficient functionality* to transition their *product increment* to the users. This may be just a small increment or a major product, but the decision is based on the fact that benefits to the user outweigh the costs of transition.

The fifth milestone is *production readiness*. That means both the product is ready for the customer and the customer is ready for the product. Remember, the goal is successful outcomes for the customer. Delivering a good product to a customer that is not ready does not fit the bill.

The final milestone may actually occur weeks or months after the project is complete, after the product has been used for some time, and the novelty has worn off; are the *stakeholders delighted* with customers successfully and happily using it? Will the customer send more business our way and be an enthusiastic advocate for us?

Systems Thinking

Closely related to governance, the Scaled Agile Framework (SAFe) suggests that organizations need to use systems thinking to be successful when performing projects in an agile manner. This organizational-level view requires a few additional techniques and organizations. The first is a *portfolio vision*. This is similar to the stakeholder vision for an individual project described previously but is less detailed and includes a description of desired future state of value streams and solutions for all of the potential projects of the organization. One tool teams sometimes use is a *value stream map*, which indicates what portions of planned work are valued by customers and what portions are not. This helps teams to consider how they are performing their work with an eye toward only doing things that customers value.

Sometimes, the work of agile teams is large, complex, and ongoing. In those cases, multiple agile teams may work together on many individual projects within a larger *program* of support and development of major systems. An ongoing team of agile teams entitled an *Agile Release Train*, which plans and works together, is needed to effectively create and maintain this portfolio vision. A release train will need to operate across geographies and regions for global organizations.

This Agile Release Train is responsible for maintaining a *continuous delivery pipeline* of useful solutions. They communicate through this pipeline with a visual depiction of workflows and activities to produce the solutions. Agile Release Trains *assume variability* between projects and teams. They preserve options to provide flexibility because of unknowns.

Initial Planning

One primary difference between agile and predictive approaches to projects is predictive projects perform most of their planning prior to performing, while agile projects plan and perform in repeated small increments or even continually. However, there is still some planning that makes sense to perform early on agile projects. We cover this aspect here, and in the next section, we cover planning that is more likely to occur repeatedly throughout the project life. While some techniques are useful in more than one way, for ease of understanding, we group them into four types of initial planning techniques. The team along with the product owner will typically use the techniques for envisioning the entire project, including what will be developed during the initiating phase of a project. The other three sets of techniques may be performed during project initiation also or early in project construction. The four sets of techniques are for:

1. Envisioning the entire project
2. Understanding user stories
3. Prioritizing requirements and work
4. Guiding improvement efforts

Envisioning the Entire Project

We cover two techniques that teams often use to envision the entire project at a high level at the outset. The first technique we cover to help a team understand the entire project at a high level goes by two different names: *story map* and *product roadmap*. There are nuances of difference between the two; story maps are sometimes told from a customer's perspective, describing what may be created overall in a project while a product roadmap can show the chronology of when different features in the project will be accomplished, including which items are being initially targeted for each release. We choose to combine the two similar techniques as a single image can be used to visualize the project including the main epics, stories within each epic and the expected release when each will be produced. Figure 7.7 shows an epic for a local government organization that wants to create an arboretum on an existing bit of land they own.

Note everything is roughly in chronological order from left to right. Also note that the top line is the *epics*—the major portions of the project. This top line is sometimes called the backbone of the project. Underneath each epic are individual stories with the higher-priority ones near the top and lower-priority ones further down. The highest priorities are collectively called the walking skeleton of the project. The project will not meet minimum acceptance without at least these being accomplished. Lower priorities are considered to be options—nice to have, but the project could be successful without them. One further aspect of the story map

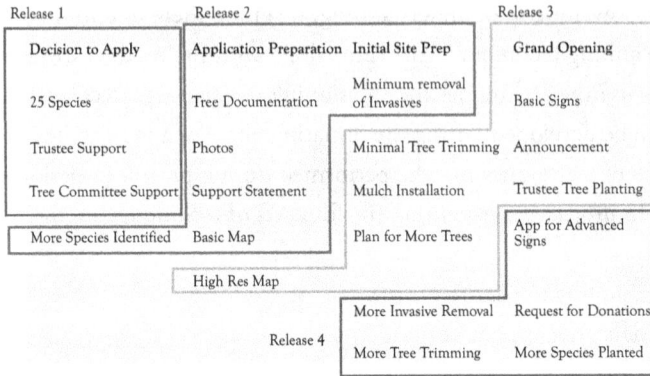

Release 1	Release 2		Release 3
Decision to Apply	Application Preparation	Initial Site Prep	Grand Opening
25 Species	Tree Documentation	Minimum removal of Invasives	Basic Signs
Trustee Support	Photos	Minimal Tree Trimming	Announcement
Tree Committee Support	Support Statement	Mulch Installation	Trustee Tree Planting
More Species Identified	Basic Map	Plan for More Trees	App for Advanced Signs
	High Res Map		
		More Invasive Removal	Request for Donations
	Release 4	More Tree Trimming	More Species Planted

Figure 7.7 Story map or product roadmap of create arboretum example

or product roadmap to note is there is a tentative marking of what will be accomplished during each release. While some projects include projected dates for each release, other projects do not. This example does not.

The second technique is a *journey map*. A journey map is a visual with simple shapes showing major portions of a project. These can be done crudely with drawing on a white board, in a sophisticated manner using software, or anywhere in between. Figure 7.8 is an example of planning a running event. With the pandemic forcing may events to be canceled, a group of friends decided to hold a socially distant 19-kilometer run as a goal to train for and enjoy a fun day. The journey map has a simple visual for each component that needs to be planned with the title of that project component underneath.

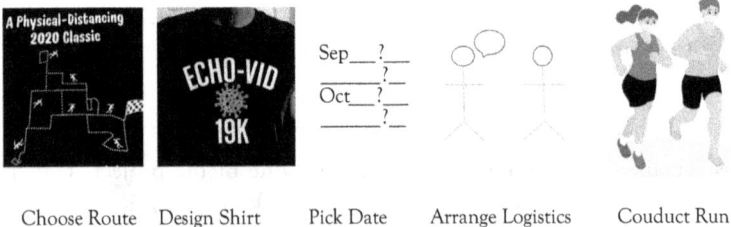

Choose Route   Design Shirt   Pick Date   Arrange Logistics   Couduct Run

Figure 7.8 Journey map example for running event

Understanding Epics and User Stories

A large desired piece of functionality or product is often called an *epic*. It is typically not defined in enough detail to produce it. An epic is small enough to be completed in one release, but often large enough that it cannot be completed in a single sprint. Therefore, it is often broken down or sliced into more detailed user stories. These stories are *sliced* or broken down into small enough portions that teams can easily envision them, estimate how much effort will be required to create them, and then commit to finishing them within a single sprint.

Slicing epics and large stories into smaller, more manageable-sized stories is the equivalent of creating a work breakdown structure (WBS) in plan-driven project management. They are similar, in that both stories and the WBS allow project participants to understand more details of a project so that they can plan and perform the required work. There are differences, however. One difference is the development team slices the stories, often each team member creating certain stories. Another difference is that stories often include a day or two worth of work, while the lowest level of detail in a WBS may be finer detail than that and may take a longer duration to develop. A third difference is that teams slice stories repeatedly throughout the project as they have more updated information and as they are preparing to work on the next sprint—they do not attempt to do this detailed planning for the entire project at the outset.

This work to understand, slice, and estimate time needed to create user stories is known as *product backlog refining*. This refinement yields *right-sized* stories, meaning they are small, understood, and the results are testable.

A *user story* is a need described by who wants it, how they are likely to use it, and why. Users are often described as personas. A *persona* may be a real, individual person by name. However, a persona is often a fictional character who has the demographics and attributes of who the expected users for the product are.

An example of how to use persona, epic, and user story is here. The persona is a 55-year-old woman who loves to garden and wants to have a new room (the epic) built as an extension of her house. She wants the added room partly so she can grow plants indoors during the winter. The team would create her epic in the form of:

As a _____

I want _____

So that I _____

Her epic would read:

As a <u>gardener</u>

I want <u>windows facing east</u>

So that I <u>can grow plants in the winter.</u>

When the team slices her epic into user stories, they may include such work as secure a permit, purchase the windows, install the electric lines, and so on. The team member who purchases the windows would likely create a list of tasks she needs to perform such as decide on the exact sizes, write specifications for energy efficiency, research possible vendors, and other tasks. The main ideas regarding epics and stories is they start with what the customer wants, and the team develops details they need to perform the work.

Two related concepts are *minimum viable product (MVP)* and *minimal marketable feature (MMF)*. While the two are sometimes used interchangeably, the purpose is different. The MVP may be a prototype used to gather understanding about how it will be accepted by customers. In our example, the MVP could be verification that during each winter month, the windows we are proposing will allow enough sunlight into key portions of the room to allow plants to grow. The MMF, on the other hand, is a single fully functional, tested feature a customer could use. Building the windows that are proven to allow enough sunlight into the new room in the winter, into the securely built room, may qualify. Extra features for the room such as built-in shelves, potting table, source of water. would not be part of the MMF as the room could be useful to the homeowner without those nice-to-have extras.

Prioritizing Requirements and Work

When scoping a traditional project, it is normal to create an extensive WBS trying to list everything that will be created and breaking it down into enough detail to estimate the cost and time to create each bit and then assign all of that work at the outset. Agile projects are different. The agile team starts with the project vision and then develops an understanding of customers and their desires written as epics. At the start, the various stakeholders may identify anything they want, and those items are added to a wish-list called a product backlog. The initial backlog may be quite daunting, but the product owner, acting as a surrogate for the customers, prioritizes that backlog by telling the team which of those epics need to be accomplished first and rejects items that are not in alignment with the product vision. A central idea in agile is to eat your desert first. What this means is the product owner selects items that will provide the most value to be created first. This *customer prioritization* is based upon input from multiple customers regarding how important and how urgently needed each item is. The idea is to create a feature that will be widely used very quickly.

There are a variety of tools agile teams sometimes use to gage customer priority. One of the more widely used prioritization tools is called *MoSCoW* which stands for:

- Must have
- Should have
- Could have
- Would like to have, but not this time

An example of MoSCoW analysis is shown in Figure 7.9.

Must Have	25 Species, Trustee Support, Tree Committee Support, Tree Documentation, Photos, Support Statement, Basic Map
Should Have	Minimum removal of Invasives, Minimal Tree Trimming, Mulch Installation, More Species Identified, Basic Signs
Could Have	High Res Map, Plan for More Trees, Announcement Trustee Tree Planting
Would like, but not this time	More Invasive Removal, More Tree Trimming, App for Advanced Signs, Request for Donations, More Species Planted

Figure 7.9 Example of MoSCoW analysis for the arboretum project

The team then breaks the higher priority epics into smaller stories. The team *refines the requirements* by gaining consensus on the *definitions of ready and done*. Ready means the team members agree that they understand a story well enough and have the necessary information, so they can effectively create it. Done means there is agreement on how the product increment will be tested and judged. By understanding in detail how the product owner will judge the product and also how the customers will use it, team members can figure out what to build how to build it, and then when they perform sprint planning, they can decide who will perform each part of the work.

Guiding Improvement Efforts

People involved in agile, whatever their role, are always trying to get better. That is why, we begin our discussion on improvement right at the start of an agile project. One key concept in improving on agile projects is to *improve collaboratively*. Team members share quite readily with each other and with stakeholders, including partial ideas and things that did not work well. They place an emphasis on learning together so that work processes, products, and people involved all get better.

We previously stated that agile teams want to create as much value as early as possible. This gains support for the team and excites the customers. One way to view value in reverse (negative value) is through considering risk. If a risk event happens, depending on how big the risk is, it can delay or even derail a project. The product owner will have all of the desired items in a product backlog but will also include risks and call it a *risk-adjusted backlog*. The bigger risks will have bigger negative value and will often be selected for completion early in the project. Therefore, agile product owners and team members sometimes decide to address a major risk head-on. That is, before doing any other work, find a way to overcome a potentially catastrophic risk. They may employ a *risk-based spike*, which is a time-boxed event of perhaps one or two weeks where the entire purpose is to test some kind of approach to make sure it will work. If it does, great! Move on to the highest priority items in the backlog. If it does not, pivot! Change your approach to one that will work.

Another technique agile teams often employ to improve right from the start is to conduct a *premortem*. This is a brainstorming description of what could go wrong on the project right as the project starts. However, the team leader often decides to role play by telling the team to imagine the project was conducted and failed and describe the failure. Then, she asks each team member to suggest multiple reasons why the failure happened and where the failure points were. The team then dissects all of these ideas and uses the knowledge they gain about what could happen to improve their planning process.

Ongoing Planning

Teams spend at least as much time in planning on agile projects as traditional ones, but much of the planning is performed in short bursts throughout the project. Much of it is delayed until the last responsible moment, so fuller information can be factored into decisions, improving the quality of those decisions. This *just-in-time (JIT) planning* is used to describe work needed for current design just when the planning is needed. Teams create small amounts of functionality often. Each bit of functionality includes tested, working product ready to deploy to users.

Teams using iteration-based agile, plan their work in releases and iterations. The *release plan* identifies what will be created in the current release and gives a high-level view of what might be produced in future releases. The team then creates a *sprint plan* in which they pick stories from that release plan, and then estimate, plan, and commit to producing those stories in the current iteration. The first release plan and first iteration plan may be created with initial planning, but subsequent ones are developed on an ongoing basis.

Product owners determine the priority of work to be accomplished and teams decide how much they can do. Team members typically plan very few weeks with over *40 hours of work*. They are trying to establish a *sustainable pace,* which they will be able to maintain indefinitely, doing high-quality work all along.

Agile participants embrace change, even late in a project. This is so different than traditional projects that are planned in detail early and then strive to rigorously control change the rest of the way. Teams on agile projects want to capitalize upon change for the benefit of the customer, recognizing both that customers change their minds, and that conditions often create the need for change. One way agile teams use change to a customer's advantage is to perform frequent *backlog refinement*, obtaining up-to-date input from stakeholders as their understanding increases, both of the deliverables being created on the project, but also of any conditions in their environment that may suggest a previously unknown variation of project deliverables may work better for them.

Summary

Agile lifecycle is based upon iterations, continuous flow, hybrid, or scaled. Progressive planning, project feasibility, project initiation, and release planning are also considered for the lifecycle. The common phases of lifecycle models are initiation, construction, and transition for iterative, Kanban, and hybrid lifecycles that were discussed in this chapter. The discussion on governance include agile metrics for success, and we considered four factors: viability and value, predictability, quality, and happiness. It is important to envision the project from a high level from two perspectives: story map or product map and journey map.

Questions

1. Of the three lifecycle models—iterative-driven, Kanban method, and hybrid lifecycles—do a comparative analysis of advantages and disadvantages. Which one is suitable for your project, and why?
2. Among the four agile metrics for success (viability and value, predictability, quality, and happiness), which is important in which phase of the project?

CHAPTER 8

Creating Useful Solutions

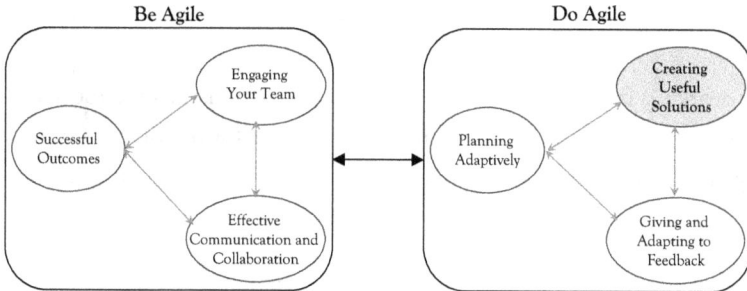

The heart of doing agile is continuous planning and solution development. Continual planning is performed at the last responsible moment, so that the team has the most accurate and up-to-date information, so they can make good decisions. When teams are using iteration-based agile, the planning and performing are conducted in a time-boxed fashion, with a regular cadence of predictability. When teams practice lean agile, people start working on a new story when they are ready and perform continued planning as needed.

At the end of this chapter, you will be able to answer:

1. What tools and metrics do you feel are most important for sprint-based agile projects?
2. What tools and metrics do you feel are most important for lean-based agile projects?
3. What three or four tools and metrics from this chapter will you plan to start using? Why those?

We start this chapter on creating useful solutions with tools and metrics for product planning. Then, we discuss tools and metrics specifically for planning increments followed by tools and metrics specifically

Table 8.1 Tools and metrics for creating useful solutions

- Product planning
- Increments
- Lean
- Continual planning
- Building
- Monitoring and controlling progress
- Quality
- Releasing

for working in a lean environment. The next sections include tools and metrics for continual planning followed by those for building, monitoring and controlling, assuring quality, and releasing product, as shown in Table 8.1.

Product Planning Tools and Metrics

The deliverables that are created in projects are called *product*. Agile places great emphasis on progressively determining what product will be produced and ensuring it satisfies customers' needs. A key concept in this progressive determination is *emergent design*, which is a gradually increasing understanding of what a deliverable will need to do and what it will include.

A *backlog* is a wish-list of things that may be created by the project team. Backlogs and increments are sometimes called *artifacts* in scrum—the things that are created or waiting to be created. If a backlog was merely a wish-list, it would be of limited value. Agile product owners, working with stakeholders and development teams, do quite a bit of prioritizing and reprioritizing the items within a backlog. In Chapter 7, we showed how tools such as a story map (also known as a product roadmap) and *MoSCoW* analysis can be used to help with prioritizing. Regardless of which tools the product owner uses, they prioritize potential work items by business value and risk. Close collaboration between the development team and the product owners will establish estimates of business value that will be viewed by many stakeholders as valid. Items that stakeholders value the most are prioritized for early construction, as are items that appear to have a major risk. The product owner first creates a *release backlog*, which is the work that is planned to be completed in current release. Then, within that release backlog, they suggest the items to be completed in the upcoming sprint. The development team then collectively decides how much work they believe they can produce during the iteration and commit to it. This is the *sprint backlog*.

User needs and desires are described as epics and stories. Each user story is described by who wants it, how they will use it, and why. Chances are the product owner has described user stories at high level initially. These are called epic user stories. They often include large functionality or product descriptions that are not defined in enough detail to estimate, plan, and produce. When this is the case, these epics are *sliced* into small stories that can be created in one sprint.

The deliverable that is created is called a product increment. This is usually more than one user story, but often less than an epic. The product increment represents the output created during an increment. The development team demonstrates how the items work. Some of the individual stories may be presented as completed, others may be presented at the *sprint review or demo* at the end of the sprint. The product owner, often with key stakeholders, decides if the items meet the *definition of done*, which is the agreement on how product increment will be tested and judged. If it is complete and works correctly, the product increment will be delivered to the proper customer. If it is not complete or does not function correctly, the item(s) in question are either returned to the backlog or the product owner may decide they are no longer needed and will not be worked on further. They may or may not be selected for construction during the next increment.

Tools and Metrics for Increments

One key aspect of iteration-based agile is that all work is completed in defined time periods and called as increments (scrum calls these sprints). These are often two- or three-week endeavors, but other time lengths are also in common use. These periods are often called *timeboxes*. Each timebox has a defined start and stop time for work to be performed. If work is not completed during the timebox, the product owner may decide to stop any more work on that item or have that be the first work to be performed in the next sprint.

The product owner prioritizes the work they most want done first, and the team decides how much they can do during the sprint and *commits to that work.* Teams need a method for estimating how much work they feel they can accomplish, so they know what they can commit to. One primary method for conducting this estimation is called *planning poker or planning games.* These are consensus tools where all team members share their opinion about how relatively large a story is in comparison to other stories they have completed in the past. As such, it is not an estimate of exactly how many hours of work will be required, but an approximation of the size and complexity. This is a method for teams to quickly size specific piece of work. They estimate the work in *story points,* which are the team members' collective best guess of how complex and large a specific story will be in comparison to other work they have previously completed. Teams often estimate crudely when they start, but after multiple iterations, they generally get quite good at determining the story points for upcoming work—a key benefit to relative sizing. The number of story points the team typically perform in an iteration is the *velocity* or speed at which they can complete story points.

One thing the teams need for this analysis is to have the stories they will complete be *right-sized*—that is, ensure each story is small, understood, and testable. Then, the team needs to estimate how many of these stories they can create in a given time period. The process of this estimating is sometimes call planning games or planning poker. This requires each story to be considered individually. Once the story has been named and questions have been answered to make sure all team members have an idea about it, all team members on a count of three vote using a card from a deck of the *Fibonacci sequence* of 1, 2, 3, 5, 8, 13, and 21. They vote about how complicated they feel the story is. These numbers do not refer to hours of work but are compared against other user stories. If most of the team members vote with the same small number such as 3 and the other member(s) voted with almost the same number such as 2, the few who voted with a different number are asked if the number the majority of people voted is okay. If so, that is the number of story points assigned. If, however, there is a very large difference in votes, the team takes time to understand each other's perspectives and revote. The typical way to understand the different perspectives is to ask one person who voted a large number and one who voted a small number to explain their thoughts. This needs to be done in a nonjudgmental fashion. Even if there is consensus about the size of a story, if it is deemed quite large (like a 13 or 21), the team usually decides to break the story down (slice the story) into two or more stories so that the work involved is better understood.

During the sprint, few, if any, changes are allowed, and great effort is expended, especially by the product owner, to allow the development team members to concentrate on their work. Remember that agile allows and encourages changes, even late in a project. Agile proponents, however, recognize that uncontrolled changes can still cause many problems. Therefore, changes can occur between sprints, but during sprints, great effort is made to continue as planned. As sprints are short, often two weeks, this means only the detailed, very short-range plans are helped constant, while anything else can change.

Tools and Metrics for Lean

As we have stated, some agile projects are conducted using a lean approach. We describe this approach first by defining what a pull production model is and the tools and metrics needed to make it work. Then, we cover the concept of flow and of reducing (or even eliminating) as many wastes as possible.

Pull Production Model

When using a lean approach, new work is not pushed to the team due to a schedule or plan. Workers only start working on a new item when they finish the previous one. This is accomplished by using a Kanban board to visually communicate the work that is complete, in process, or waiting to be started, and only starting a predetermined number of items until some of them are complete. A *Kanban board* is a visible information radiator that openly communicates work status for everyone to see. Kanban boards will be discussed in Chapter 9 with other communication tools.

There are several understandings people need to make a lean system work. One is to *optimize the whole* system. That means teams look at what the whole system needs, not just what makes it easier for them. To gain understanding of what is best for other projects or portions of their project, teams need access to transparent and open exchange of information, including draft ideas, and partially complete work. Another key concept for making lean work is to *build quality into everything* that is done. Without proper quality, workflow is reduced, and waste and mistakes are increased. Further, as work is planned and performed on a *just-in-time* basis, if any partial work is not at the correct quality, the product cannot be used, and it slows everything down. Finally, as the work is pulled through only when needed, *decisions can be deferred* until the last responsible moment when the team has the most information.

Flow

Lean agile methods have a continuous workflow with highly visible information. Workers pick the next work item off a prioritized list once they finish the previous item. The continual nature of the workflow enables:

- Extremely rapid response to changing demands
- A stream of new functionality to be delivered quickly
- Feedback to be given just as quickly
- An ability for each worker to concentrate on one thing at a time and avoid the task switching waste of multitasking.

When creating a lean environment, the team make process rules explicit. This ensures everyone understands how a process works. As the people are performing work within the process, they strive to improve collaboratively. When one person has problems, others help, and the workers learn together. While the team members may have been selected initially because they were good at one thing (specialists), through this process of helping each other out, they become *generalized specialists*—very good at one thing, but also fairly competent at a wide variety of work that is needed.

A big part of lean systems is managing workflow. Teams focus on reducing time to complete work. While multiple measures are sometimes used in an effort to control the time for production, the two most common are throughput and cycle time. *Throughput* is the average number of units produced during a time duration. When using iteration-based agile, this could be either the number of units per iteration or the number per unit of time such as per week. When using lean agile, it is always per unit of time. Throughput tells how many units of work the team is finishing per time period. A goal is to be able to complete a fairly consistent amount of work (be predictable) so that stakeholders can count on you. Teams find the best ways to maintain or increase this is to divide work into small stories and a consistent batch size that everyone understands and to utilize other good work practices such as waste reduction strategies discussed next.

A related measure is *cycle time,* which is the time from when work starts on an item until it is delivered. The shorter the cycle time, the more a team is able to be responsive to customers. When cycle time is long, there is more partially completed work. This is called *work in progress* or WIP. One method for reducing WIP is that once a person starts work on one item, works on it continuously until it is complete. Allow as few interruptions as possible. One key role of the team leader is to reduce those disruptions so that the team members can work with great focus on the item they started. A second method for shortening the cycle time is to identify and remove bottlenecks. A *bottleneck* is something in the work process that limits the amount of work that can be completed. Some bottlenecks are easy to identify such as a machine that can produce a set number of items per hour. Other bottlenecks can be much more difficult to identify; however, through careful observation and measurement of work, teams can often find the bottleneck that limits the amount of work they can produce. Once identified, the team tries to find a way to increase the amount of work that can go through the bottleneck part of the process. Work to improve parts of the process that are not the bottleneck will not speed up the process. Only speeding up the slowest part speeds up the whole.

Eliminate Waste

When striving to produce faster, less expensive, and better solutions, anything that either slows down progress, causes mistakes, or costs extra money is not valued by the customer. Lean agile teams define the minimum amount of features a solution or portion of a solution needs and determine everything beyond that is waste. Those minimal necessary features constitute the *minimum viable product (MVP)*.

The goal is to reduce or even completely eliminate waste when possible. By working deliberately on waste reduction, teams can little by little make their work processes more efficient. Lean proponents describe multiple types of waste, as shown in Chapter 7 and as follows. Each type of waste can increase time and cost and/or reduce quality of our deliverables. For example, someone invested time to create partially done work (also known as WIP). The WIP is not yet of any value and, if with updated feedback, a decision was made to pivot the direction of the project, the WIP may never be of value. It represents cost, but not value. For a second example, if the team creates extra features that are not needed, they spent time (and therefore cost) in creating those features. By including more features, they added to the complexity of the product, which increases the chance that some interactions between features will create a failure (reduce quality). Each of the other wastes negatively impact time, cost, and/or quality.

WIP	WIP costs worktime, is not yet of value, and may be obsolete
Extra processes	Steps such as extra documentation or planning that add no value
Extra features	Extras not used by the customer add cost and failure possibility
Task switching	Time and concentration are lost when changing workflow
Waiting	Delays may mean later feedback and task switching
Handoffs	Whenever work is turned over, some tacit knowledge is lost
Defects	Incorrect work must be found and corrected quickly

Continual Planning

While some of the planning techniques described earlier occur primarily early in a project, the ones described here often occur repeatedly throughout the project interspersed with continued work creating the solution. One key driver of all of this ongoing planning is a commitment to deliberatively capture and share tacit knowledge. Tacit knowledge is often informal and only in the head. To make good decisions, that knowledge needs to be made explicit and shared openly. One key driver of willingness to openly share informal knowledge is trust. If members do not trust each other and their leaders, they will be unwilling to share. To enhance this trust, a good team leader shows personal vulnerability, asks when they need help, and do what they say they will do. This role modeling encourages other team members to also share openly.

For example, teams plan at multiple levels. At the outset, planning is high-level, capturing the project vision and little else. As the project proceeds, releases are planned at a bit more detail, then sprints are planned in yet more detail. Team members share daily and even more often what they are working on, enabling other team members to perform very detailed planning for their own work. Ideally, teams perform as much of this planning as practical in a collaborative manner both to capture the best ideas and to increase motivation, transparency, and to make knowledge explicit. Team members continuously identify risks, using specific feedback. The product owner seeks to progressively understand true needs and uses that knowledge to continually refine requirements.

Build

Building is creating the products and services the customers want. This effort ideally makes up a large percentage of the time team members spend on a project. On any project, stakeholders want to know how things are progressing, and agile is no different. There are several tools and concepts used in agile to determine and communicate status.

Iteration-based agile teams build in a regular, repeating pattern of iterations with a set length of time-boxed effort. While two weeks is the most typical length for iterations, both shorter and longer iterations are sometimes used. Each iteration has a *cadence,* which is a rhythm of planning, performing, demonstrating, and reflecting on the work of one sprint after another. For example, before starting an iteration, team members need a definition of ready for each story they are asked to create. That definition of ready is an agreement that the team members understand the story well enough to satisfy it. Both in planning for and performing the work of an iteration, team members strive to identify any impediments—things that can interfere with a team member doing their work. One role of the scrum master is to remove impediments so that the team members can focus on productive work. At the end of an iteration, when work results are being demonstrated and the team reflects in their retrospective, the team and their product owner may elect to continue according to the current release plan, stop work entirely, or pivot. A *pivot* is a change in direction on the next sprint usually based upon customer desires, but potentially based upon the effectiveness of work performed to date.

Monitoring and Controlling Progress

It is essential to monitor progress on any project, and agile projects use some of the same techniques as predictive projects and some unique techniques. One concept is that of *information radiator.* These are highly visual displays of work with whatever supporting information is needed to interpret the display. We show several of these information radiators in Chapter 9. Ideally, the information displayed will be so obvious that little or no added explanation is needed. The goal is not to convince anyone about how smart the team is, but to help everyone interested to clearly understand the status of the project.

The most useful information to understand progress is often not isolated numbers, but one set of numbers in comparison to another. Two examples are variance analysis and trend analysis. *Variance analysis* is a quantitative review of any differences between what was expected and what actually occurred. Has the project done more work, less work, or about what was expected? *Trend analysis* is a quantitative review of changes in performance over time. Is work progress getting better, worse, or remaining about the same over time. Armed with answers to these questions, teams and product owners (and other decision makers) can sometimes determine to continue, to pivot, or to cancel work on a project.

Status of work on agile projects are often communicated via *burn-up* or *burn-down* charts. These are line graphs that show both estimated work and actual remaining work for burn-down charts and estimated work and actual completed work for burn-up charts. The burn-up charts will look vaguely familiar to people who know earned value analysis. Related to the burn-up chart is the *cumulative flow diagram*. That is a visual information radiator that shows total, in progress, and completed work over time. These three types of charts are shown in Chapter 9 with other communication tools.

Quality

XP has promoted a number of practices that help to ensure the solutions that are developed work properly. Some of these ideas come directly from XP, and others have their roots in the total quality movement that are updated and included in XP. While these tend to be aimed specifically at IT projects, we seek to broaden their application to any agile projects with a little adaptation.

It starts with *test-driven development.* That is the practice of determining test to be used before writing code. Understanding how project deliverables will be judged before starting to create them is useful on any project. One key in agile projects, of course, is this is performed repeatedly as more information is known. At multiple points, the tests for acceptance of the next deliverable or set of deliverables can be determined before building those deliverables. Three other ideas from XP are related. *Verification and validation* are ensuring quality at multiple levels and time periods, through various tests. *Continuous integration* is the practice of immediately ensuring each bit works in the overall system. *Refactoring* is simplifying and cleaning code to make it stable and maintainable. On any type of systems project, as new bits of output are integrated into the system, opportunities can arise to simplify and improve the overall system that were not envisioned at the start of the project. Collectively, these four ideas can be applied to any project to ensure work is understood before it is started, tested in appropriate ways as soon as possible, and needed adjustments are immediately made.

Once work has started, again, XP has two ideas for working together that are useful on any agile project. *Pair programming* is the practice of one programmer writing, while another reviews the work. Carried out continuously, it can be exhausting as one is either creating code or very closely monitoring that development. The benefits of working so closely together are that team members learn from each other and mistakes are found quickly, increasing initial quality. Team members discuss details of approaches, and both know so much more detail about what is being created. *Collective code ownership* means all team members are responsible for code that is being developed, and any team member can change it. This is a powerful concept both for accountability and empowerment. If there is anything wrong with the product, all team members share responsibility. Every team member is trusted enough to both make changes and to communicate those changes to her teammates.

No talk of quality would be complete without discussing how to find and overcome problems. A technique that comes from total quality management of a generation ago is the *five whys*. This quality technique is composed of striving to find the root causes of problems by asking questions. Typically, the effects of a problem are more obvious than the causes are, and by uncovering one cause, a deeper probing can find that there are more underlying causes. There is nothing magic about the number five, but the point is to keep asking why until it no longer makes sense.

1. Why do we have this error? Because we tried to work too fast.
2. Why did we try to work too fast? Because we needed this part to go with another part.
3. Why was the other part ready first? Because we did not share during our stand-up meeting and we did not know it.
4. Why did we not share at the stand-up meeting? Because that team member was out.
5. Why was that team member out? Because of being home sick.

Defects are errors and bugs to software and any other problems with whatever output we are producing. The *defect rate* is how many of these we find. Hopefully, we find most of them before we turn over work at the end of an increment or before we turn in work when completed in lean agile projects. It is more disruptive and expensive if we discover the problems after work is transferred—especially to an external client. These are called *escaped defects*.

Release

When we complete construction, we are ready to transition our deliverables to our client. The *release decision* is based upon the readiness of our product, our support, and our customers. We first determine the *minimum marketable release (MMR)* for our deliverables. That is, what are the features and functions that are useful enough to our customer that their value is greater than the cost of transitioning them? The trend is to transition many small improvements, but there is a cost of transition. Part of the cost is internal in terms of *support readiness*. Can we provide the instruction, service, and anything else needed to ensure our customers can successfully use the product we have created for them? The other part of the cost is external. *Customer readiness* means the customer knows what the product will be and is prepared to accept and use it effectively. The last phase in our project lifecycle is called *transition*, not something simpler like closing. It is transition because we are taking a relationship approach with our clients, not a transaction approach. Our goal is not to merely create and deliver according to specific technical specifications. Our goal is to help make our customer successful using the product we create in close cooperation with them. We have sought their feedback early and often. We have made many changes, sometimes even drastic pivots, in response to their evolving understanding. Now we transition our deliverables to them in such a manner that we help them become successful.

Summary

This chapter discusses about tools for product planning both for agile with sprint-based life cycles and for lean-based lifecycles. It includes tools for working with backlogs, speed, flow, risks, and quality. The chapter includes many suggestions for building useful solutions, monitoring and controlling progress, ensuring and improving quality, and releasing product to customers once both product and customers are ready.

Questions

1. What tools and metrics do you feel are most important for sprint-based agile projects?
2. What tools and metrics do you feel are most important for lean-based agile projects?
3. What three or four tools and/or metrics from this chapter will you plan to start using? Why those?

CHAPTER 9

Giving and Adapting to Feedback

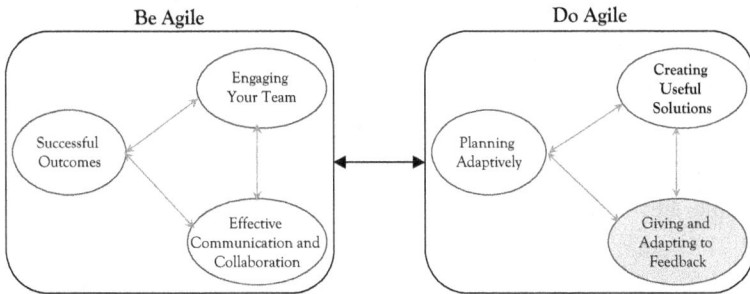

Appropriate time and content of the feedback is integral to the agile method as requirements evolve and as the project moves from one phase to the other and from one sprint to the other. Agile must adapt to delivering value to the client in a fast-changing environment. Feedback assumes greater importance as agile embraces this concept of change and ability to change. The agile manifesto requires client or customer collaboration all the time, and timeliness is ensured to some extent for this reason.

At the end of this chapter, you will be able to:

1. Describe major types of visual communication in agile and tell why they are important.
2. Describe five main events in agile and the desired outcomes of each.
3. Describe testing in agile and when each type is used.
4. Describe four main types of agile contract clauses and why each helps both parties.

Need for Feedback

Frequent feedback is essential for agile projects for several reasons. Agile projects require close collaboration between the project team and the client. It is evident from earlier discussions that the agile method follows an iterative process to realize business value, which is not necessarily clear at the outset. Therefore, along with close collaboration, frequent interactions with the client help the project team to get clarity about the project outcome and enhance business value. For this reason alone, it is necessary that the agile process adapts short feedback loops. Regular and continuous feedback from the business key stakeholders such as the client and end-user are essential to develop correct solutions and enhance business value incrementally. Such a frequent feedback from the client and end-users helps the agile team to stay focused on the desired outcomes that enhance business value.

These short feedback loops also help the project team to manage changes to the project during the project development phase as the feedback discussions help *share knowledge* by identifying new requirements and modify existing requirements to enhance business value. It is for this reason the agile process incorporates built-in deterministic check points to facilitate frequent feedback.

The daily standup (scrum calls it daily scrum) less than 10 to 15-minute meetings are meant to share status updates and identify obstacles. This can be accomplished by asking questions such as what was done yesterday, what is planned for today, and are there any risks or technical issues than can hold back the work progress. As you might have realized, this stand-up meeting itself is part of the feedback process. The first question, "what was done yesterday" provides feedback on what was done well and what went wrong. In the process, future action plan will be determined as an outcome of these meetings.

A feedback loop cycle happens after every sprint. The sprint events also present an opportunity to identify and discuss what about the increments that can be delivered and tested. This incremental process creates a process of feedback at every stage of product development. As a result, the project team receives feedback on the current product or solution and identification of unfulfilled needs of the client. However, sometimes, waiting till the sprint is complete could be a problem, as a minor misstep in the early stage of a process may result in a major problem, and fixing it would be time-consuming and cost-prohibitive. So, it is important to have feedback even during the sprint and as frequently as possible, albeit for a short duration in a day. In the case of software development agile projects, visual communication plays an important role due to the technical nature of the project.

Agile project teams usually work at a quick pace because of the nature of the business and the level of competition in global market. The absence of frequent and accurate feedback could result in developing solutions that are erroneous and may lead to rework, which increases cost and time. Ideally, the feedback—as a project team consists of people representing diversity in culture and different generations—must happen in person. Face-to-face interactions readily facilitate questioning everything, a fundamental value to agile process. Further, in a face-to-face meeting, the scrum master can manage the team dynamics and discussions to focus on the issue, ensure that feedback is accepted based on merit, minimize emotions, control ego-related obstructions, contribute to solving the problem at hand, and support participation and open discussions (not arguments).

When an agile project is managed by multiple teams that are colocated or geographically dispersed, the feedback becomes a challenge, and it becomes even more complex when project teams work with contractors. Video conferencing is a possible alternative to provide and receive feedback. As nonverbal communication is absent for the most part, visual feedback prior to or during the videoconferencing may facilitate effective feedback and communication.

Frequent interactions and open feedback with the team improve cohesion and collaboration among the team members. Teams can come up with better and more innovative solutions to enhance business value to the client.

Visual Communication

As the famous saying goes, a picture is worth thousand words. In general, agile projects deal with abstract problems that are not clear either to the client or the development team. A big picture or gestalt cannot be

Develop Iteratively   Provide Frequent Feedback

Focus on Business Value

AGILE approaches

Build Incrementally

Collaborate with Client

Provide Servant Leadership

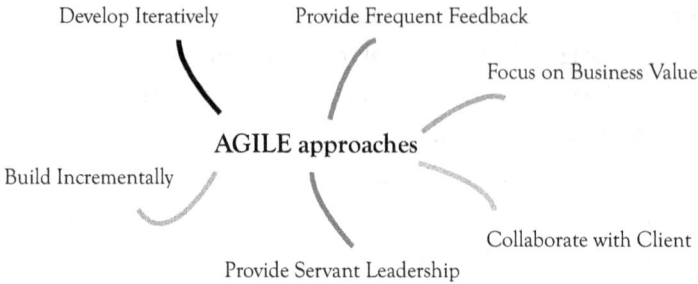

Figure 9.1 Information radiator

formed easily. In the absence of a big picture or clarity about the project deliverables, visual communication is desirable. Visualization of a problem or an attempt to visualize the problem adds clarity to the problem and will help in solving it.

From early days of childhood, when language skills are not developed, children learn from visual messages. This is a fundamental learning trait that stays with us throughout our life. In social media like Facebook and Twitter, many popular users attach importance to visual images to convey their message. Often you will find posts or tweets with visuals get more attention and acknowledgements with likes, shares, and retweets. This learning trait can even be effectively used for agile teams.

Compared with verbal communication, a big advantage of visual communication is that it takes a short duration to convey the message effectively. Visual communication conveys a message that you might not have realized before through verbal communication. And, at a glance, the visual image conveys more information, facilitates easy discussion, and supports participative decision making. In the process, knowledge sharing among the participants would be an additional advantage, as an image brings out tacit knowledge (Figure 9.1).

Visual communication is accomplished through an *information radiator*[1], which is a visual device that conveys project information publicly in the workplace. Information radiators are essential components of visual management and are popular in agile projects. Popular information radiators include storyboards, a variation called Kanban boards, burn-down charts, and burn-up charts.

---

[1] A popular term invented by Alistair Cockburn.

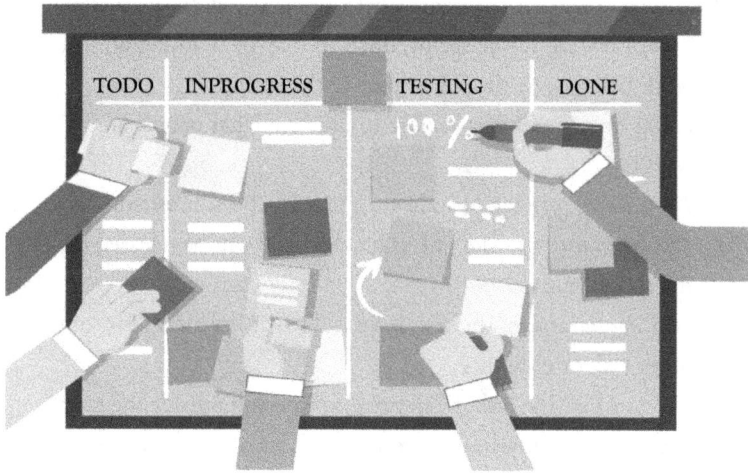

Figure 9.2 Storyboard

Storyboard

Managing visually involves presenting information using visualization techniques to manage work and communicate with the team. Often, a simple tool that is popular among agile teams is sticky notes on a *storyboard* to present tasks with their status (to do, in progress, or done), and sometimes relations among them (predecessor and successor relations) and/or other information. A good storyboard should be easy to read and use (Figure 9.2).

Further, the employed project methodology should depend on it for monitoring and executing the project, as otherwise, the project team would perceive it as an extra burden or duplication of work. Therefore, some level of standardization is required for the storyboard. The value of the task board is realized only when it is updated daily and used for monitoring on a daily basis. A storyboard should be kept alive and up to date. A storyboard can employ several elements such as:

- *One-day tasks*: Limit tasks to one day to show daily progress and flow.
- *Status tags*: Colored post-it note to indicate the status.
- *Three columns*: Columns for to do, in progress, and done.

- *Unplanned items and legacy issues*: The first row for tasks that do not belong to the sprint, but you may be working on. All work being done should be part of the sprint.
- *Name tags*: Small post-it note to indicate what people are working on.
- *Done status tag*: Tag to indicate a task has been finished.
- *Blocked status tag*: The task is blocked and can be released by the scrum master.
- *Waiting status tag*: The task is on hold as it is waiting for some other task or clearance.
- *Delegate tag:* The task is delegated to a person outside the team.
- *Analyze tag*: An indication to the product owner that more information is needed.

Done status can also be denoted using a star symbol, and these tags are removed during the daily scrum and celebrate the successful completion of the task. The daily stand-up meeting takes place in front of the storyboard, and the storyboard is the source of information for daily stand-up meetings. One may also post pictures of team members along with or in lieu of their names on the storyboard. If multiple teams are engaged in the project, each team is assigned a color theme, and these colors are used to identify and distinguish teams or a program board may be used for this purpose. The board that aligns multiple teams is normally called a program board. It is very similar to traditional project management, with the biggest difference is that it is now an information radiator.

Each team will have a storyboard and inter-relations, and dependencies of teams can be shown on a higher-level storyboard, which is sometimes referred to as scrum of scrums. Some of the visible and obvious benefits of a storyboard are:

- Team members enjoy working on it and updating it.
- The daily standup meeting gives an opportunity for team's visual interaction.
- People from the organization who pass by get updated information about the project.
- Status reports to senior management is simplified.

- Regular updates during the day creates synergy and motivation to work harder.
- Easy to understand even for anyone who did not see it before.
- Simple and does not need explanation.
- Waste of time in communicating and collaborating is reduced drastically.
- It is fun and looks great.

In essence, a task board is an excellent tool for visual communication, feedback, and for promoting collaboration and effective communication.

Kanban Board

One version of task board is Kanban. Research shows that many visual management ideas are adapted from traditional Lean thinking and Toyota Lean Production System based on customer demand. The underlying principle is to minimize waste and maximize value to the customer. As agile focuses on offering business value to customers while minimizing rework, it is often considered an agile project management tool. Kanban boards are designed to visualize work and use cards and columns for people to visualize and commit to the work.

Kanban is a Japanese concept of managing workflow management. It is designed with an intent to visualize work, maximize efficiency, and be agile in executing the work. Kanban is a billboard or signboard in Japanese language.

Like many other tools, agile teams adapt Kanban, a concept that is originated from manufacturing. With three basic work-related groups like *To Do*, *In Progress*, and *Done*, a Kanban concept presents a real-time progress information and identifies bottlenecks that are likely to interrupt working practices and processes (Figure 9.3).

The cards that are placed on a Kanban board are usually written as tersely as possible—an example of a savage summary. They could be as simple as two words such as *create interface* or *update list*. They cards may have a bit more detail, perhaps including the initials of the team member who will perform it. The cards, however, are often by design very brief and are merely the first part of a *3C process* of card, then conversation

TO DO	IN PROGRESS	Done

Figure 9.3 Kanban board

about them, and finally, a confirmation that there is common understanding of the task.

Four foundational principles of Kanban work very well with the agile method. In fact, they summarize the agile approach:

1. Start with what you do know.
2. Agree to pursue incremental and evolutionary change.
3. Respect the current process, roles, and responsibilities.
4. Encourage acts of leadership at all levels.

In addition to these four principles, some of the practices of the Kanban also support agile methods very well. Practices such as visualizing the workflow, limiting the work in progress, explicitly stating policies, relying on feedback loops, and improving the value collaboratively align with agile practices. Because of this, Kanban can be used in conjunction with an agile method without disrupting its processes.

Visual communication is simple and less susceptible to misinterpretation. Visual communication is also perceived to be fun, and colorful images are stress relievers too. For these reasons, visual communication can influence attitude and behavior. Visual communication also promotes transparency and trust among the team members.

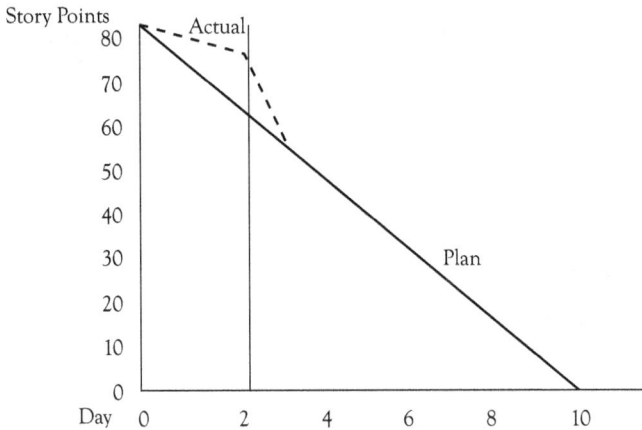

Figure 9.4 Burn-down chart

Burn-Down and Burn-Up Charts

Yet another common information radiator used in agile is to show progress in relation to the total amount of work that is needed. This is often accomplished by a *burn-down chart,* which starts at the total amount of planned work for an iteration and works toward zero. Alternatively, one could start at zero and work their way up toward to the total amount of work expected visually presenting this as a *burn-up chart* and is most often seen as a release burn-up chart.

Figure 9.4 is an example of a burn-down chart with an iteration of two weeks (10 workdays) and a plan for a steady cadence of completing eight story points per day on the average. The dashed line represents work actually completed. Note that the first couple of days, the actual line was behind the expected line, but caught up on Day 3. This shows the team is making expected progress overall. The team will continue to post their progress each day, and because this chart is visible for any stakeholder to see, they are being very transparent. This increases trust and predictability.

Events (AKA Meetings or Ceremonies)

Agile now generally uses the term events for what in many other situations would be called meetings and for what agile used to call ceremonies. We will use the current agile terminology of events. Five main

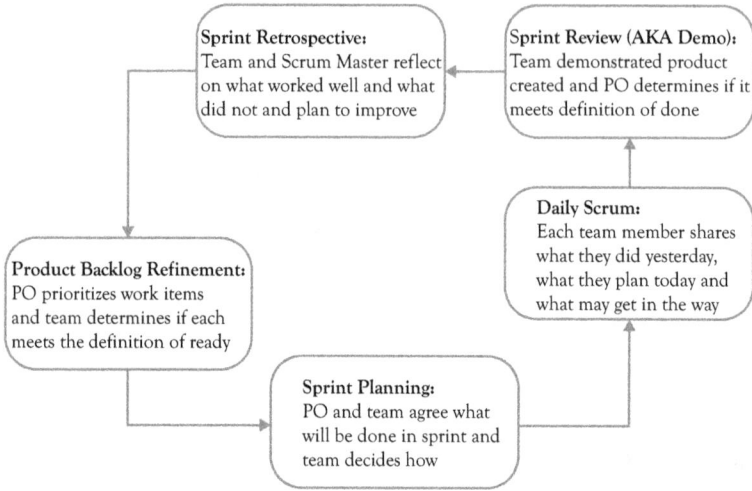

Figure 9.5 Agile events

events are planned for each sprint in scrum, and they are product back-log refinement, sprint planning, daily standup, sprint demo, and sprint retrospective. The four are depicted in Figure 9.5.

- *Product backlog refinement:* A planning meeting to understand, slice, and estimate the time to create each user story to ensure each meets the definition of ready.
- *Sprint planning:* A planning meeting to plan the work outputs and methods for the upcoming sprint.
- *Daily scrum:* A 15-minute meeting for each team member to share what they did yesterday, what they plan today and what may get in the way.
- *Sprint review (aka demo):* A demonstration meeting when the team shows product created and product owner (PO) deter-mines if it meets definition of done.
- *Sprint retrospective:* A review meeting in which the team and scrum master reflect on what worked well and what did not and plan to improve.

Product Backlog Refinement

Remember that a *product backlog* is a wish-list of any and all work that might be created by a project team during a project. This list is continually being refined partly by shifting customer desires as they better understand their needs and as conditions change. The product owner also refines the backlog by prioritizing items within it. The team helps to refine the backlog by asking questions, slicing large epics and stories into stories small enough to be well-understood, and a definition of ready agreed upon. The *definition of ready* is an agreement that team understands a story enough to bring into a sprint. This implies that the team understands the *definition of done,* which is the agreement on exactly how the PO will judge the deliverables produced. It also implies that after the team has estimated the work that will be entailed, they feel each story selected can be completed during the upcoming sprint.

Sprint Planning

Sprint planning is to celebrate the completion of the previous sprint and planning for the next sprint. Usually, the product owner, scrum master, and development team attend this ceremony. This meeting is an opportunity for the product owner to also discuss the prioritized list of backlog items that might be considered in the next sprint. The team members then select stories from the sprint backlog, estimate, plan, and commit to the work they will complete during the sprint. The team relies upon their experience and judgment to determine how much work they feel they can commit to completing. A term teams like to use to describe this is "yesterday's weather." A common joke with a ring of truth regarding weather forecasts is to predict today's weather, just plan for the same as yesterday. Likewise, teams know that if they are in a rhythm, they are likely to be able to do about the same amount of work in the upcoming sprint as they completed in the last sprint. Teams will often use planning games as described in the previous chapter to help them estimate.

Daily Standup

The daily standup is discussed earlier in this chapter. The time limit of 15 minutes and stand-up meeting convey the importance of focusing on only important issues and utilizing time effectively. Each team member would answer the three questions (what did I do yesterday, what will I work on today, are there any obstructions or *impediments* to my work?), and usually, the meeting is held at beginning of the workday. This is an open meeting, and all interested stakeholders are welcome to listen; however, they do not get a speaking role. This meeting is designed to promote productivity, accountability, and responsibility of every development team member. If the development team members are geographically dispersed, tools such as videoconferencing and virtual group chats are employed for this meeting. These meetings are not a time to debate issues or to diagnose problems. If one team member knows something that may help another with planned work for the day or an obstruction, they will often make eye contact and then talk after the meeting, so time is not lost in the meeting with everyone else just listening to two people talk. The team leader makes notes of all of the obstructions and individually works with team members offline to overcome them.

Sprint Review (AKA Demo)

The sprint review or demo, which takes place after the sprint is complete, is a forum for each team member to showcase new features or discuss significant accomplishments during the sprint. Apart from the product owner and team leader, people in attendance may include other teams and project stakeholders. The product owner makes the determination as to whether each story is complete to her satisfaction. Sprint review is considered complete when the work is accepted. The previously agreed-upon definition of done is the standard for this judgment. If items are deemed to be satisfactorily complete, they are transitioned from the team. If not, they go back into the backlog and may or may not be selected for the next iteration.

Sprint Retrospective

A sprint retrospective happens after sprint demo, to discuss and analyze what worked well and what needs improvement. One of the agile core values is continuous improvement and the sprint retrospective is aimed for that purpose. In this ceremony, a restraint must be placed to control complaints and accusations and focus on finding creative solutions to overcome impediments. Team members sometimes do not see the value in retrospectives unless they see positive changes made in future sprints.

For this reason, one strategy is to pick the low-hanging fruit first. That is, choose one or two obvious possible improvements and focus on doing them well in the very next sprint. Likely, many ideas will surface, but by focusing on one or two at a time, visible progress is more likely to be achieved. Remember, the improvement can be to the process of doing the work, the people who are doing the work, and product that is created. Wise team leaders, by asking probing questions, use different methods of soliciting input in retrospectives to keep it fresh. They also are mindful that some people quickly offer ideas, while others do not, so some methods of capturing ideas by voice and others of capturing ideas in writing also help to get everyone actively participating.

These five ceremonies are part of the scrum process to create a team pace to optimize productivity, encourage collaboration, and sustain transparency with a purpose to inspect and adapt throughout the project and facilitate continuous learning. They also serve as effective feedback mechanism for the agile team, product owner, scrum master, and all other key stakeholders.

Testing

Testing is to ensure that the deliverable meets requirements, and it also serves as an important feedback mechanism. For agile projects, we generally hear about the guiding principle of preferring working software over comprehensive documentation. However, it is not necessarily true with testing practice, and some documentation may be necessary.

Testing is planned early. One popular current agile concept is to *shift left*, meaning perform as much testing and get as much feedback as soon as possible, so needed changes can be implemented quickly and work to be redone will be minimized. Testing is conducted often to ensure that any unsatisfactory work is discovered quickly and to further ensure that everything produced works seamlessly together. As many systems can be quite complicated, ensuring all portions work effectively together is critical. Unlike in traditional projects, it is not necessary that testing takes place only after a major work element of deliverable is complete. It usually is a continuous integration of development and testing, specifically for software development. Consequently, a test plan is written and updated for every release. The test plan provides team members an understanding of how their work will be judged as acceptable before they start on their work. It is so much easier for a person to perform quality work if they understand exactly how it will be judged. A typical test plan includes:

- Scope of the testing
- Functionalities considered for testing
- Type of test
- Test of performance
- Inclusion of infrastructure issues
- Risk mitigation
- Resources

The first phase of testing happens in the project initiation stage that will focus on establishing and testing boundary conditions or limits to the scope of delivery, architecture, and risks. Based on these elements, a cost estimate is developed.

During the second phase of development, the construction phase, important and major portions of testing take place. During this stage, there could be multiple releases and many iterations. Two aspects of testing take place during this stage; *confirmatory testing* to ensure that requirements or intent of the stakeholders is fulfilled and *investigative testing* to identify problems or ignored requirements. Specifically, investigative testing plays an important role as feedback, as it deals with testing of integration, load or stress, and security. Confirmatory testing includes developers testing it first and then acceptance testing with the client, which serves as an important feedback. Testing is performed at multiple levels such as:

- *Unit test*   Ensuring a small function works properly
- *Integration test*   Ensuring new functionality works immediately in an existing system
- *Acceptance test*   Verifying for customer that the entire system works correctly

During the third or transition phase, the system is deployed. This phase provides critical feedback to the client and end-users. During this phase, end-users are trained, operational people are supported with relevant information, and user documentation is provided. This phase often mulls over product release, related marketing, backup, and system finalization.

Testing in agile requires continuous involvement of testers, and often, they also help the development team in their daily development activities. Inadequacy in preparing for a test plan is a common issue that one must have to overcome. As requirements and updates are frequent and inherent in any agile project, it would remain a challenge for testers. As a remedy to this situation, testers should be included in all the iterations, and they should remain active members of the feedback system.

Problems

One of the problems with agile implementation is the level of understanding of the agile method across all levels of the organization. According a study by Rigby et. al (2016), executives do not go through agile training, and they do not really understand the agile method. As a result, they manage in traditional ways that are not aligned with agile principles and practices. Obviously, effective implementation of agile method suffers. For example, executives may opt for more initiatives violating the agile approach of focusing on prioritizing the work. They may also assign people to multiple projects. From a feedback point of view, executives may ask for more meetings, thereby interrupting the development work. In a worse scenario, they may promote ideas that were rejected by the development team and introduce more control processes to monitor work. Consequently, the agile process will be in quandary.

Another problem is application of agile across the board. It is not a solution for any project. Agile is best suited for software innovation where many things such as requirements and possible outcomes are unclear. However, agile is not applicable where parameters are relatively stable and routine. If requirements can be clearly defined, agile should not be applied for that project. Agile is most suitable when problems are complex, and solutions are not known. Applying agile to other projects is a problem.

When agile professionals in the organization are not competent enough, not self-motivated, not innovative, and the team is not self-managed, the agile methodology should not be employed. But, once an organization has an agile professional team that is equipped with all desirable traits, it should allow the agile team to develop norms and processes and customize their practices depending on the project at hand. Of course, continuous improvisation is the responsibility of the agile project team, and the team may continue to innovate and improve agile processes and practices to suit the problem at hand, with an ultimate goal of enhancing business value to the customer. Past research suggests that stable teams are more productive and more responsive to customer input than transient teams and stability is important for agile teams as well. But, do they stay together for long? This is where executives must demonstrate understanding of the agile method and act accordingly. Rigby et al. (2016) quote that scrum alliance found that more than 70 percent of the agile practitioners report tension between their teams and the rest of the organization. This is a problem that must be addressed. All these problems can be addressed well if there is a systematic, routine, open, and transparent feedback system in place for the entire organization. Agility in thought and action are important for success.

Agile Contracts

As agile projects do not have a clear specification at the outset, there is a need, as we have discussed throughout this book, to have development teams and stakeholders work collaboratively and iteratively together. Standard contracts, especially firm fixed-price contracts, do not lend themselves to motivating that needed cooperation. Consequently, several types of contract clauses have been developed that do encourage cooperation. Four of the most common include:

- Change for free
- Money for nothing
- Graduated fixed price
- Fixed price work packages

Change for free is a contract term that says if the product owner attends every meeting the team wants him or her to, then the product owner can make a change in direction. In other words, the product owner can pivot at the end of one increment and ask the team to do different work than originally planned at a high level. The product owner is the person who can decide what work is the highest priority to be done next (but, of course, the team decides how much they can do in a given iteration). This change for free clause is what allows an agile project to change direction without going through a change control process.

Money for nothing is a type of cost sharing arrangement. It means that if there is a fixed-price contract, but the product owner decides the work remaining is not necessary, they can stop work. The team gets a previously negotiated percentage (say 20 percent) of what they would have earned for the work if they did it, and the buyer pays just for the work actually done plus that small percentage for the work they originally thought they needed. Once again, the product owner needs to attend all of the requested meetings. This clause enables an agile project to stop once the remaining work is not worth the remaining cost.

Graduated fixed price is another cost sharing arrangement. If the team gets the work done in less time than expected, they get a higher hourly rate. If they get it done as expected, they get the standard hourly rate. If they take extra time, they get lower than the normal hourly rate. This clause gives the team an incentive to do their work promptly and correctly. It gives both buyer and seller the same incentive.

Fixed price work packages are just as the name implies. The contract prices the project in chunks, instead of the entire project. The buyer then chooses which work packages are desired and only pays for them.

Improving

Continuous improvement is a norm for growth-oriented organizations that strive to improve their competitive advantage in the marketplace. However, improvement invariably follows an incremental and iterative approach. Before an improvement is thought of, it is important to have an understanding of the process wherein the improvement is proposed.

Initiating	Diagnosing	Establishing	Acting	Learning
Set context	Define desired state	Set priorities	Create solutions	Analyze and validate
Build sponsorship	Develop	Develop approach	Plan/test solution	Propose future actions
Charter infrastructure	recommendation	Plan actions	Pilot/test solution	
			Refine solution	
			Implement solution	

Adapted from SEI, 1986

Figure 9.6 Improvement process

Adapted from SEI, 1986.

A minor or major improvement idea is conceived in the context (process) where such improvement is targeted. Software Engineering Institute (SEI) Capability Maturity Model suggests an approach of finding a sponsor to implement the idea, understanding the infrastructure, defining desired results, and then making recommendations. The team improvement process is shown in Figure 9.6.

Once a recommendation is accepted, the agile team must set priorities, develop an approach to implement the improvement idea, and plan its implementation. Solutions are created and pilot tests are conducted in the next phase. The results of the pilot test helps the team to refine the solution, analyze and validate results after implementation, and then plan on further improvements in the next cycle. This improvement cycle usually takes anywhere between two and six weeks.

As is true to product delivery, during every sprint, the sponsor or the product owner also develops and prioritizes an improvement backlog, and these improvement ideas are taken up based on the set priority. This priority is based on the benefit and value of the improvement idea. Participation of the development team is key to this improvement process. Changes and improvements do not produce positive results instantly. It will take time to record productivity improvements.

Summary

Agile projects are conducted with a team working collaboratively with their scrum master, product owner, and various stakeholders. A central tenant of agile is to start with the project vision and progressively learn as work is being performed. This requires openness to feedback and ideas. Teams use visual communication, various types of meetings (called ceremonies), testing, and specific contract clauses to motivate, give, receive, and effectively use feedback. Collectively, these things help to adapt a project to serve the customer.

Questions

1. Describe major types of visual communication in agile and tell why they are important.
2. Describe five main events in agile and the desired outcomes of each.
3. Describe testing in agile and when each type is used.
4. Describe four main types of agile contract clauses and why each helps both parties.

CHAPTER 10

Agile in a Nutshell

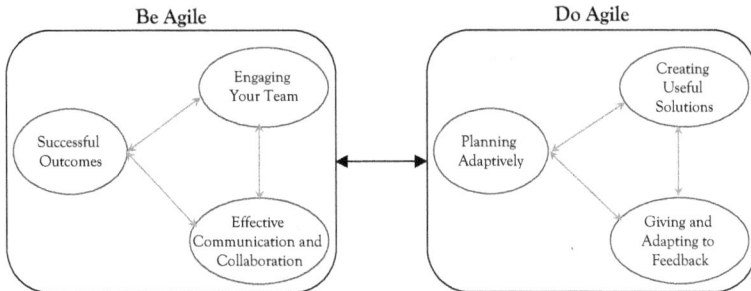

Many projects are conducted using either pure agile or a hybrid of some sort, with agile being part of the method. There are many approaches to agile, some using different terminology and some interpreting the same in a different manner. There are also competing credentials in agile. Many people understand either one approach or parts of agile generally. Further, many websites and consultants offer advice.

The purpose of this book is to cut through the clutter and describe agile in a simple, yet in a complete and comprehensive manner. Chapters 2 and 6 go into details of what agile approach promotes both the mindset ideas (Chapter 2) and the techniques and metrics (Chapter 6). Chapters 3 through 5 describe how to *be agile* fits neatly into three broad and interrelated topics: understanding successful outcomes, engaging your team, and communicating and collaborating. Chapters 7 through 9 describe how to *do agile* also fits into three broad and interrelated groups of techniques: planning adaptively, creating useful solutions, and giving and adapting to feedback.

Figure 10.1 shows how these six components of agile are related. The next few sections of this chapter form an outline that shows a bit of detail regarding each of the six areas. The final section of this chapter suggests a few ways to combine a mindset idea from Being agile with a technique or

Be Agile   Do Agile

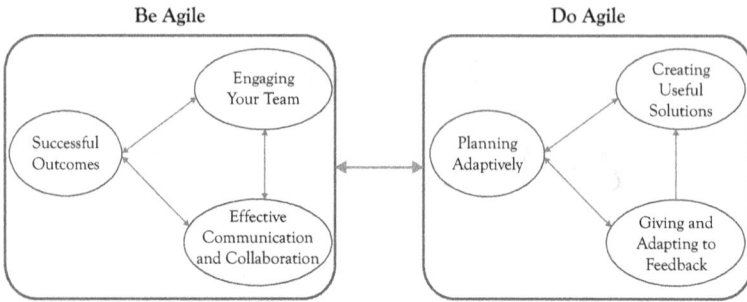

Figure 10.1 Agile in a nutshell

two of doing agile. There are certainly many more combinations of being and doing agile, but we wanted to give you a few ideas to consider.

Be Agile

Successful Outcomes

- Customer-driven vision
- Customer-driven value
- Simplicity
- Excellence
- Improvement

Engaging Your Team

- Leadership
- Leading agile teams
- Team development and motivation
- Decision making
- Team roles

Effective Communication and Collaboration

- Transparency
- Feedback
- Timeliness

Do Agile

Planning Adaptively

- Agile lifecycles
- Governance
- Systems thinking
- Initial planning
- Ongoing planning

Creating Useful Solutions

- Product planning tools and metrics
- Tools and metrics for increments
- Tools and metrics for lean/Kanban
- Continual planning
- Build
- Monitoring and controlling progress
- Quality
- Release

Giving and Adapting to Feedback

- Need for feedback
- Visual communication
- Meetings (aka events or ceremonies)
- Testing
- Problems
- Agile contracts
- Improving

Ideas for Being and Doing Agile Together

Through this book, we have encouraged you to think about the mindset, principles, and values that underlie agile as you perform some of the techniques and use some of the metrics to assess how you are doing. Here we offer you a handful of ideas how to combine the two. We use the outline of mindset topics, including methods of leadership and primary roles, and briefly describe two techniques of metrics for each.

Product Vision

An agile project starts with a *product vision,* which describes customer satisfaction and alignment with business objectives at an initially high level. This product vision gives the development team an understanding of how the envisioned product will be used and what a successful outcome will be for the customer. One method used to aid this understanding is the *persona,* which is a fictional username, description, and values for the solution. By being able to envision a person who needs the output of the project, teams can often better satisfy those needs. A second method to help with understanding and achieving the product vision is *product backlog refinement,* which is a planning meeting to understand, slice, and estimate the time to create each user story to ensure each meets the definition of ready. This promotes a more detailed understanding of specific features that comprise the product so that each can be created successfully.

Customer-Driven Value

Customer-driven value defines value from a customer's perspective. The only work customers care about is work that directly adds value to the solution a team creates for them. One technique that promotes this is a *product roadmap,* which is a visual showing high-level plans of products expected to be created during each release. This aids communication between the customer and the developers by showing at a high level what capabilities are planned for development during each release. Customers can ensure that everything planned is something they want and value. A second useful technique for delivering customer-driven value is *acceptance testing,* which is verifying for customers that the entire system developed works correctly. Solutions are only valuable when they work.

Simplicity

Simplicity is doing what is needed and no more, taking small simple steps, using the sheerest possible design to meet today's requirement.

The concept of simplicity is central to agile in both planning and execution. Do not do anything that is not needed or in a more involved manner than necessary. One tool that aids simplicity is the *40-hour work week,* which is a plan to work at sustainable pace. Projects are very often under time pressure from stakeholders who are eager to use the solutions being developed. The very reason for a project is someone needs the results, and they want them quickly. There may be a need to temporarily work overtime, but if a team must consistently work overtime, they tend to burn out and have quality problems. Working at a sustainable pace is a simplicity idea that helps teams be effective in the long run. A second useful simplicity technique is identifying and dealing with *bottlenecks.* A bottleneck is the portion of a work process that limits amount and speed that can be accomplished. By identifying bottlenecks and finding a way to relax the hold they have on the work process, a team can accomplish more work.

Transformational Leadership

Transformational leadership occurs when a leader aims to develop trust and align personal values of individuals (followers) to accomplish vision and mission of the organization. When a product owner works with a team to create a *project charter*, the team aligns with the goals of the project and understands how the project goals support the overall organization. As such, team members know the work they are doing is important and why. This is quite motivating. A second technique that is helpful is *continued viability,* which is composed of one or more milestones during the project construction stage to ensure the team is still making progress. This is not only a chance for the team to self-diagnose, but also to receive feedback on the amount and quality of their work and how the solutions they are developing remain consistent with stakeholder needs.

Servant Leadership

Servant leadership occurs when a leader focuses on needs of the followers first. The leader may accomplish this through integrating followers' needs with project goals, honesty, delegation, and empowerment. Servant leaders realize their primary role is to help their followers become successful. One technique agile servant leaders use is the *definition of ready*, which is an agreement that team understands a story enough to bring into a sprint. Servant leaders use these definitions to make sure team members are not forced to start work that may be impractical, risky, or too large for a given sprint. By encouraging team members to openly agree after discussion that they understand what is required to accomplish a story, they set the team up for success. A second technique servant leaders use is to deal with *impediments,* which are things that can interfere with team members doing their work. By removing impediments, servant leaders enable team members to spend a higher percentage of their time accomplishing needed work.

Emergent Leadership

Emergent leadership occurs when different team members informally take on leadership roles at different times and are supported by team members and other stakeholders. A key aspect of agile is team members accomplish much of the planning, organizing, coordinating, and controlling that a project manager may perform in a more command-and-control-type environment. For team embers to step up to this challenge requires leaders to create the culture and trust team members need to believe they are truly being encouraged. One technique used by emergent leaders is the *daily scrum (aka standup)*. This brief meeting, usually conducted each morning, is where each team member shares what they did the day before, what they plan to do today, and problems or impediments they envision. This allows each team member to take accountability for their work, but also to communicate with the rest of their team. Often, after the meeting, two team members will confer on a particular work plan or impediment. Another method emergent leaders use is *collective code ownership* in which all team members are responsible for code, and any member can change it. When each member feels responsible for the product and can take action to improve it, leaders emerge.

Product Owner

The *product owner* is the person who represents the client or customer and other stakeholders, prioritizing work and making timely decisions, enabling an agile project team. Almost every worker wants to do good, useful work. Two related difficulties with that is not always knowing what the customer wants and needs in detail and not having a person with authority making timely decisions. A key role of product owners is *customer prioritization,* which is to make timely decisions on the importance or urgency of work based on customer input. This person has frequent contact with a whole range of stakeholders and is available to the agile team when needed. Near the time or transitioning product to customers, another technique product owners use is to assess *customer readiness.* This is when product owners determine if the customer knows what the product will be and is prepared to accept and use it effectively. This important work is a reminder that successful customer outcomes is the goal, not just turning over deliverables.

Scrum Master

The *scrum master* is the person who facilitates and guides the team to improve performance, removing roadblocks, so the members can focus on their work. Scrum masters practice servant leadership and may spend more of their time handling obstacles for team members than creating actual product themselves. One technique scrum masters use is managing *handoffs.* A handoff occurs whenever work is turned over from one worker or group to another and some tacit knowledge is lost. Astute scrum masters seek to capture that tacit knowledge and make it explicit. This both helps make the handoff more seamless, and it is useful in improving future work. A second technique scrum masters help facilitate is to *manage flow,* which is when teams focus on reducing time to complete work. Smoother workflow often yields better product as without interruptions, workers can concentrate better.

Team Member

Team members are people who work on a project in cooperation with others to develop the solution for the stakeholder. A key aspect of agile teams is they are proactive, not passive. The members take active roles in planning and performing their work. One key tool they use is *committing to work.* This is when the team promises how much they will accomplish in timebox—whether that is a sprint, a spike, or an event. For a sprint, the team members will ensure they understand each story the product owner has prioritized using their definition of ready. They will determine how much work they can accomplish and commit to it. Then, they will strive earnestly to accomplish that work. Team members also *improve collaboratively*. That is, when one worker has problems, others help and learn together. This sometimes takes place during a sprint when one worker has a problem and others stop their work to help. It also takes place sometimes during *retrospectives* as team members work together to identify lessons learned, and plan to improve people, process, and product.

Transparency

Transparency occurs when all people openly present the facts as they are to create necessary trust. If agile teams and product owners are expected to make good decisions, they need to have accurate information that they can rely on. Information is viewed as a resource to be openly shared to help everyone do their work and make necessary decisions. This is so opposite of the cynical view of using information as power to only share when it is to one's advantage. One technique to increase transparency is to *make processes explicit,* which is to ensure everyone understand how a process works. This is often performed by team members standing in front of a white board with markers and sticky notes as they describe for each other how and why they do something. Teams use many variations of *information radiators,* which are highly visual devices that convey project information publicly in the workplace. By thus enabling all stakeholders to see what is happening, trust increases, decisions are made more promptly, and work quality improves.

Feedback

Feedback is used to demonstrate results early, listen carefully, and make adjustments as needed. Early and frequent feedback is a key value in agile, as initial planning is only at a high level, and as customers gain better understanding both of their work environment and of the possibilities the project can create, they can make better decisions of what they need.

One technique agile teams use for obtaining feedback is *objective milestones*. These occur as decision points based on objective evaluation of progress toward working systems. We identified six types of milestones starting with understanding the *product vision* and demonstrating a *proven approach*. Early in a project to *customer readiness* near the end of the project. A second technique agile teams use to obtain feedback is a *sprint review (aka demo)*. This is a demonstration meeting when the team shows the product they created, and the product owner determines if it meets definition of done. Agile teams use these milestones and reviews to gain needed feedback so that they can continue work as planned, pivot to new work or new approaches, or stop work that is no longer needed.

Future Trends

We made a humble effort to cover agile concepts and promising practices and techniques comprehensively in this book. As is true with an agile approach, we believe these practices and techniques will continue to evolve for better. Agility will remain a tenet for the agile method, and we will continue focus on future trends in agile and adapt them as they deem fit. As is true with PMI updating PMBOK, which is now organized to emphasize principles, and other project management-related standards routinely and regularly, we firmly believe the agile method will certainly take a similar path of progression, with an ultimate goal of delivering products and services faster, better, and cheaper.

Bibliography

Agile Alliance. 2019. "Agile Glossary." https://agilealliance.org/

Agile Business Consortium. 2017. "Culture and Leadership: The Nine Principles of Agile Leadership." https://agilebusiness.org/page/Resource_paper_nineprinciples (accessed on September 1, 2020).

Allue, X.Q. 2009. "Kanban Board." http://xqa.com.ar/visualmanagement/2009/06/kanban-boards/ (accessed on July 21, 2020)

Ambler, S. et al. 2018. "Extending the Agile Manifesto – 2018." https://projectmanagement.com/blog-post/61955/Extending-the-Agile-Manifesto—2018 (accessed on September 1, 2020).

Anantatmula V. 2010. "Project Manager Leadership Role in Improving Project Performance." *Engineering Management Journal* 22, no. 1, pp. 13–22.

Anantatmula V. 2016. *Project Teams: A Structured Development Approach,* ISBN-13: 978-1-63157-162-6. Business Expert Press.

Anantatmula, V. 2008. "Role of Technology in Performance Model." *Project Management Journal* 39, no. 1, pp. 34–48.

Anantatmula, V. 2008. "Role of Technology in Project Manager Performance Model." *Project Management Journal* 39, no. 1, pp. 34–48.

Anantatmula, V. 2010. "Leadership Role in Improving Project Performance." *Engineering Management Journal* 22, no. 1, pp. 13–22.

Anantatmula, V. 2016. *Project Teams: A Structured Development Approach.* ISBN-13: 978-1-63157-162-6. Business Expert Press.

Arnold, R.D., and J.P. Wade. 2015. "A Definition of Systems Thinking: A Systems Approach." *Procedia Computer Science* 44, pp. 669–678.

Author not known (n.d.) "Kanban Explained for Beginners: The Complete Guide." https://kanbanize.com/kanban-resources/getting-started/what-is-kanban (accessed on July 21, 2020)

Author not known (n.d.) "What is Agile Testing? Process, Strategy, Test Plan, Life Cycle Example." https://guru99.com/agile-testing-a-beginner-s-guide.html (accessed on July 23, 2020)

Author not known (n.d.). "Visual Management Blog." http://xqa.com.ar/visualmanagement/2009/02/visual-management-for-agile-teams/(accessed on July 21, 2020)

Backlander, G. 2019. "Doing Complexity Leadership Theory: How Agile Coaches at Spotify Practice Enabling Leadership." *Creativity and Innovation Management,* https://onlinelibrary.wiley.com/doi/full/10.1111/caim.12303 (accessed on September 1, 2020).

Bancroft-Conners, J. 2020. "Agile Metrics: 4 Balanced KPIs to Measure Success." https://appliedframeworks.com/agile-metrics-4-balanced-kpis-to-measure-success/ (accessed on September 1, 2020).

Basusourav. 2015. "12 Core Practices of XP." https://basusourav.wordpress.com/2015/05/18/12-core-practices-of-xp/ (accessed on September, 2020).

Bjorn, W. 2018. "Scrum Values: Commitment." https://explainagile.com/agile/scrum/values/commitment/ (accessed on September 1, 2020).

Shea, C. 2015. "The Agile Bear Inspirations: Episode 6: Respect." https://solutionsiq.com/resource/blog-post/the-agile-bear-inspirationsepisode-6-respect/ (accessed on September 1, 2020).

Bonebright, D. 2010. "40 Years of Storming: A Historical Review of Tuckman's Model of Small Group Development. https://tandfonline.com/doi/abs/10.1080/13678861003589099 (accessed on October 23, 2010).

Bridges, M. 2019. "Scaled Agile Framework: An Overview of its Core Values, Principles, and Implementation." https://medium.com/@mark.bridges/scaled-agile-framework-an-overview-of-its-core-values-principles-and-implementation-f6357c5c5e41 (accessed on September 1, 2020).

Casanova, S., et al. 2019. "Agile in Enterprise Resource Planning: A Myth no More." https://mckinsey.com/business-functions/mckinsey-digital/our-insights/agile-in-enterprise-resource-planning-a-myth-no-more (accessed on September 1, 2020).

Crawford, M. 2016. "5 Lean Principles Every Engineer Should Know." https://asme.org/topics-resources/content/5-lean-principles-every-should-know (accessed on September 1, 2020).

David J. Anderson School of Management. 2020. "The Principles and General Practices of the Kanban Method." https://djaa.com/the-principles-and-general-practices-of-the-kanban-method/ (accessed on October 9, 2020).

DevIQ. 2020. "Courage: Take Pride in Your Code." https://deviq.com/courage/ (accessed on September 1, 2020).

Digital.ai. 2020. "What is Agile Methodology?" https://digital.ai/resources/agile-101/agile-methodologies (accessed on September 1, 2020).

Dybå, T., and T. Dingsøyr, T. 2008. "Empirical Studies of Agile Software Development: A Systematic Review." *Information and Software Technology* 50, no. 9, pp. 833–859.

Dybå, T., and T. Dingsøyr. 2008. "Empirical Studies of Agile Software Development: A Systematic Review." *Information and Software Technology* 50, no. 9, pp. 833–859.

Eary, J. 2018. *Agile Working and the Digital Workspace: Best Practices for Designing and Implementing Productivity.* New York, NY: Business Expert Press.

Extreme Programming. 2020. "Agile in a Nutshell: The Practices." http://agilenutshell.com/xp (accessed on September 1, 2020).

Fadi, S. 2016. "MVP vs. MMF – What's the Difference?" https://excella.com/insights/mvp-vs-mmf-whats-the-difference (accessed on September 1, 2020).

Foegen, M., M. Solbach, and C. Raak. 2009. "Agile Process Improvement." https://resources.sei.cmu.edu/asset_files/Presentation/2009_017_001_22328.pdf (accessed on July 24, 2020)

Forte, F. 2020. *Agile Thinking Demystified*. New York, NY: Business Expert Press.

Francino, Y. 2020. "Modern Agile and Heart of Agile: A new focus for agile development." https://techbeacon.com/app-dev-testing/modern-agile-heart-agile-new-focus-agile-development (accessed on September 1, 2020).

Ghahrai, A. 2019. "What are Scrum Ceremonies in Agile?" https://devqa.io/scrum-ceremonies/ (accessed on July 22, 2020)

Github. 2014. "XP Simplicity Rules." https://wiki.c2.com/?XpSimplicityRules (accessed on September 1, 2020).

Goodman, D. (n.d.) "Agile Process: Why You Need Feedback Loops Both During and After Sprints." https://mendix.com/blog/agile-process-why-you-need-feedback-loops-both-during-and-after-sprints/#:~:text=As%20part%20of%20its%20focus,they%20deliver%20high%2Dvalue%20features (accessed on July 09, 2020)

Greenleaf, R. 1998. *The Power of Servant Leadership*. San Francisco: Berrett-Koehler Publishers, Inc.

Griffiths, M. 2015. *PMI-ACP Exam Prep: A Course in a Book for Passing the PMI Agile Practitioner (PMI-ACP) Exam*. Minnetonka, MN: RMC Learning Solutions.

Hoogveld, M. 2018. *Agile Management: The Fast and Flexible Approach to Continuous Improvement and Innovation in Organizations*. New York: Business Expert Press.

Kalra, D. 2017. "Lean Software Development—7 Wastes of Software Development." https://agilecoachdiaries.wordpress.com/2017/01/19/lean-software-development-7-wastes-of-software-development/ (accessed on September 1, 2020).

Kanbanize. 2020. "What is Continuous Improvement? Definitions and Tools." https://kanbanize.com/lean-management/improvement/what-is-continuous-improvement (accessed on September 1, 2020).

Kelly, J. 2014. "The Importance of Emergent Leadership." from: https://sites.psu.edu/leadership/2014/09/07/the-importance-of-emergent-leadership/ (accessed on June 26, 2020)

Kendis. 2018. "How SAFe Core Values Stabilize and Accelerate the Progress of Agile Teams?" https://kendis.io/scaled-agile-framework/safe-core-values-stabilize-accelerate-progress-agile-teams/ (accessed on September 1, 2020).

Kittler, M., D. Rygl, and A. Mackinnon. 2011. *Special Review Article: Beyond culture or beyond control? Reviewing the Use of Hall's high-/low-context concept*. Sage Perspectives. https://journals.sagepub.com/doi/abs/10.1177/1470595811398797 (accessed on October 23, 2020).

Klein, K.J., J.C. Ziegert, A.P. Knight, and Y. Xiao. 2006. "Dynamic Delegation: Shared, Hierarchical, and Deindividualized Leadership in Extreme Action Teams." *Administrative science quarterly* 51, no. 4, pp. 590–621.

Kloppenborg, T., V. Anantatmula, and K. Wells. 2018. *Contemporary Project Management*, 4th ed. Cengage Learning.

Kloppenborg, T.J., and L.J. Laning. 2012. *Strategic Leadership of Portfolio and Project Management: Bridging the Gaps Between Setting and Executing Strategy.* New York, NY: Business Expert Press.

Koskela, L., and G. Howell. 2002. "The Underlying Theory of Project Management is Obsolete." *Project Management Institute*, 293–302. Proceedings of the PMI Research Conference: Project Management Institute.

Koskela, L., and G. Howell. August, 2002. "The Theory of Project Management: Explanation to Novel Methods." *In Proceedings IGLC*, 10 vol, 1–11.

Lean Enterprise Institute. 2020. "Principles of Lean'" https://lean.org/whatslean/principles.cfm (accessed on September 1, 2020).

Lean Sensei. 2020. "Value Innovation: Value from the Customer's Perspective." https://leansensei.com/2013/08/value-innovation-value-customers-perspective-2/ (accessed September 1, 2020).

Lines, M., and J. Smart. 2020. *Choose Your WoW!: A Disciplined Agile Delivery Handbook for Optimizing Your Way of Working (WoW).* Newtown Square, PA: Project Management Institute.

Michigan Technological University Office of Continuous Improvement. 2020. "What is Lean?" https://mtu.edu/improvement/learn/what/ (accessed on September 1, 2020).

Mitchell, I. 2017. "Walking Through the Definition of Ready." https://scrum.org/resources/blog/walking-through-definition-ready (accessed on October 19, 2020).

Nicolaas, D. 2018. *Scrum for Teams: A Guide by Practical Example.* New York, NY: Business Expert Press.

Paquette, P., and M. Frankl. 2016. *Agile Project Management for Business Transformation Success.* New York, NY: Business Expert Press.

Piikkila, J. 2020. "What is SAFe?" https://atlassian.com/agile/agile-at-scale/what-is-safe (accessed on September 1, 2020).

Planview. 2020. "Lean Principles 101 Guide." https://planview.com/resources/guide/lean-principles-101/ (accessed on October 7, 2020).

Plays in Business. 2020. "Agile Games." https://plays-in-business.com/agile-games-facilitation/ (accessed on October 8, 2020).

Project Management Institute. 2014. "PMI Agile Certified Practitioner (PMI-ACP)® Examination Content Outline." https://pmi.org/-/media/pmi/documents/public/pdf/certifications/agile-certified-exam-outline.pdf?v=225d4b98-7500-4707-908a-07695fe21d38&sc_lang_temp=en (accessed on September 1, 2020).

Project Management® Institute. 2017. *A Guide to the Project Management Body of Knowledge PMBOK® Guide 6th Edition*. Newtown Square, PA.

Project Management Institute. 2017. *Agile Practice Guide*, Newtown Square, PA.

Project Management Institute. 2017. *Agile Practice Guide*, Newtown Square, PA.

Project Management Institute. 2020. "A Hybrid Toolkit'" https://pmi.org/disciplined-agile/hybrid-framework (accessed on September 1, 2020).

Project Management Institute. 2020. "Governing Agile Teams." https://pmi.org/disciplined-agile/people/governing-agile-teams (accessed on September 1, 2020).

Rigby, D.K., J. Sutherland, and H. Takeuchi. 2016. "Embracing agile." *Harvard Business Review* 94, no. 5, pp. 40–50.

Rogers, T. and V. Anantatmula. 2018. "Project Teams for Traditional and Agile Projects: Why are They Different? *International Journal of Engineering Research and Applications* 8, nos. (10-II), pp. 1–14.

Rogers, T., and V. Anantatmula. 2018. "Project Teams for Traditional and Agile Projects: Why are they Different?" *International Journal of Engineering Research and Applications* 8, nos. 10-II, pp. 1–14.

Scaled Agile. 2019. "Scaled Agile Core Values." https://scaledagileframework.com/safe-core-values/ (accessed on September 1, 2020).

Scaled Agile. 2020. "Built-In Quality." https://scaledagileframework.com/built-in-quality/ (accessed on September 1, 2020).

Scaled Agile. 2020. "SAFe Lean-Agile Principles." https://scaledagileframework.com/safe-lean-agile-principles/ (accessed September 1, 2020).

Schuurman, R. 2017. "Tips for Agile Product Roadmaps and Product Roadmap Examples." https://scrum.org/resources/blog/tips-agile-product-roadmaps-product-roadmap-examples (accessed on September 1, 2020).

Schwaber, K., and J. Sunderland. 2017. "The Scrum Guide: The Definitive Guide to Scrum: The Rules of the Game." https://scrum.org/resources/scrum-guide (accessed on October 7, 2020).

Scrum Alliance. 2016. "The Three Pillars of Empiricism (Scrum)." https://scrum.org/resources/blog/three-pillars-empiricism-scrum (accessed on September 1, 2020).

Scrum Alliance. 2017. "Maximize Scrum with the Scrum Values: Focus." https://scrum.org/resources/blog/maximize-scrum-scrum-values-focus-part-1-5 (accessed on September 1, 2020).

Scrum Alliance. 2020. "Scrum Values." https://scrumalliance.org/about-scrum/values (accessed on September 1, 2020).

Scrum.org. 2020. "Scrum Glossary." https://scrum.org/resources/scrum-glossary (accessed on September 1, 2020).

Sironi, G. 2013. "XP Values: Communication." https://dzone.com/articles/xp-values-communication (accessed on September 1, 2020).

Srivastava, N. 2015. "Scaling Agile." Retrieved on March 07, 2020 from: https://pmi.org/learning/library/develop-agile-approach-with-these-tips-9888

Stone, A.G., R.F. Russell, and K. Patterson. 2004. "Transformational Versus Servant Leadership: A Difference in Leader Focus." *Leadership & Organization Development Journal.*

Tolbert, M. 2020. *Hybrid Project Management: Using Agile With Traditional PM Methodologies to Succeed on Modern Projects.* New York, NY: Business Expert Press.

Tuckman, B.W. 1965. "Developmental Sequence in Small Groups." *Psychological Bulletin* 663, no. 6, p. 384.

Tuckman, B.W., and M.A.C. Jensen. 2010. "Stages of Small-Group Development Revisited." *Group Facilitation: A Research & Applications Journal* 10, pp. 43–48.

Tutorialspoint. 2020. "Extreme Programming – Values and Principles," https://tutorialspoint.com/extreme_programming/extreme_programming_values_principles.htm (accessed on September 1, 2020).

Vanderjack, B. 2015. *The Agile Edge: Managing Projects Effectively Using Agile Scrum.* New York, NY: Business Expert Press.

Varhol, P. (n.d.) "To Agility and Beyond: The History—and Legacy—of Agile Development." https://techbeacon.com/app-dev-testing/agility-beyond-history-legacy-Agile-development (accessed on May 20, 2020).

Vineyard, S. 2016. "Story Map vs. Product Roadmap." https://excella.com/insights/story-map-vs-product-roadmap (accessed on September 1, 2020).

Visual Paradigm. 2020. "Definition of Done vs. Acceptance Criteria." https://visual-paradigm.com/scrum/definition-of-done-vs-acceptance-criteria/ (accessed on September 1, 2020).

Wade, S. 2017. "The Importance of Visual Communication for Software Testing Teams." https://agiletestingdays.com/blog/the-importance-of-visual-communication-for-software-testing-teams/(accessed on July 16, 2020)

Waters, Kelly. 2011. "Lean Principle #7 – Optimize the Whole." https://101ways.com/2011/03/11/lean-principle-7-optimise-the-whole/ (accessed on October 7, 2020).

Wells, D. 2009. "Simplicity is Key." http://extremeprogramming.org/rules/simple.html (accessed on September 1, 2020).

Wells, D. 2009. "The Values of Extreme Programming." http://extremeprogramming.org/values.html (accessed on September 1, 2020).

Wikibooks. 2020. "Software Engineering with an Agile Development Framework/Iteration One/System Metaphor." https://en.wikibooks.org/wiki/Software_Engineering_with_an_Agile_Development_Framework/Iteration_One/System_metaph or (accessed on September 1, 2020). https://scrum.org/resources/scrum-glossary (accessed on June 16, 2020).

Savage Summary Glossary

Acceptance test	Verifying for customer entire system works correctly
Adaptation	Continually improve based upon inspection
Advocate for agile	Modeling agile behaviors, discussing values, and educating stakeholders
Agile	(aka change-driven) a project method using iterative and continual processes, guided by an empowered mindset described in the Agile Manifesto and elaborated by many sources
Agile coach	A person who guides team members in learning to work more effectively by collaborating with each other and who promotes agile in the broader organization.
Agile lifecycle	Iteration-based production of solutions including inception, construction, and transition phases
Agile Release Train	Ongoing team of agile teams that plans and works together
Agility	The ability to move quickly and easily responding to changing customer desires
Artifacts	Backlogs and product increments
Assume variability	Preserve options to provide flexibility because of unknowns
Bottleneck	The portion of work process that limits amount and speed
Build quality in	Workflow is reduced and waste increased if mistakes are made
Burn-down chart	A visual presentation that starts at the total amount of planned work for a sprint and works toward zero

Burn-up chart	A visual presentation that starts at zero and work their way up toward to the total amount of work expected
Cadence	The rhythm of planning, performing, and evaluating each sprint
Change for free	Agreement allowing customer to substitute future work packages
Charter project	Ensure all stakeholders have a common understanding and are committed
Collective code ownership	All team members are responsible for code and all can change it
Commit to work	Team promises how much they will accomplish in timebox
Commitment	Team follows through, only take on tasks they can do
Communication	Confer on everything, every day, create best solution together
Construction phase	Incremental planning, delivery, and feedback until release-ready
Continued viability	Milestone(s) through construction to ensure team is making progress
Continuous delivery pipeline	Visual depiction of workflows and activities to produce solutions
Continuous improvement	Pursue perfection by enlisting all in never-ending effort to get better
Continuous integration	The practice of immediately ensuring each bit works in system
Continuously identify risks	Specific effort to use feedback and engage team to identify risks
Courage	Tell the truth, work together, adapt to changes, question status quo, have difficult conversations
Culture	Behaviors and beliefs that are characteristics of a particular social, ethnic, or age group.

Cumulative flow diagram	Visual information radiator that shows total, in progress, and completed work over time
Customer prioritization	Decide importance or urgency of work based on customer input
Customer readiness	Customer knows what the product will be and is prepared to accept and use it effectively
Customer-driven value	Define value from a customer's perspective
Cycle time	The time from when work starts on an item until it is delivered
Daily scrum (aka standup)	Brief meeting where member shares what is done, what is planned, and problems
Defect rate	How many errors and bugs are found in product created
Defects	Incorrect work must be found and corrected quickly
Defer decisions	By making decisions as late as possible, teams have better information
Definition of done	Agreement on exactly how the PO will judge the deliverables produced
Definition of ready	Agreement that team understands a story enough to bring into a sprint
Delighted stakeholders	Milestone at end of transition when product is successfully used with trained and happy users
Disciplined Agile Delivery (DAD)	Agile approach that supports various lifecycles and emphasizes measurable outcomes and scaling
Duration	The time-boxed length of sprints such as one or two weeks
Earned value	Number of story points completed versus expected in time period
Embrace change	Acceptance and eagerness to serve updated customer needs

Emergent design	Gradual understanding of the shape of a deliverable
Emergent leadership	Different team members informally take on leadership roles at different times and are supported by team members and other stakeholders
Empiricism	Work in a fact-based, experienced-based manner
Encourage emergent leadership	Create a safe environment where team members promote each other into influential opportunities
Epic	Large functionality or product, not defined enough to produce
Escaped defect rate	Errors and bugs that have escaped from the task of creating product and may be found internally or externally
Events	Five types of meetings titled backlog refinement, sprint planning, daily scrum, sprint review, and sprint retrospective
Experimentation	Encourage individuals and teams to try, perhaps fail, and share lessons
Extra features	Extras not used by the customer add cost and failure possibility
Extra processes	Steps such as extra documentation or planning that add no value
Extreme Programming (XP)	Agile approach that emphasizes technical methods and feedback
Feedback	Demonstrate results early, listen carefully, make adjustments
Five whys	Quality technique striving to find the root cause by asking questions
Fixed-price increments	Agreement to pay set amount for current increment of work
Focus	Teams finish what they start, limit work in progress (WIP)

Forty-hour work week	Plan to work at sustainable pace
Generalized specialists	Very good at one thing, but also fairly competent at a wide variety of work
Graduated fixed price	Agreement by which a contractor makes more if completed early
Handoffs	Whenever work is turned over some tacit knowledge is lost
High-context culture	Communication patterns in which we must understand everything in the situation as much meaning is derived from unspoken words and unwritten rules
Hybrid	Some hybrid approaches combine agile and plan-driven or two different agile approaches such as lean and scrum
Impediments	Things that can interfere with a team member doing their work
Improve collaboratively	When one worker has problems, others help and learn together
Information radiator	Highly visual device that conveys project information publicly in the workplace
Initiation phase	Time from project idea until vision agreed and okay to commence (essentially the same as initiating stage in plan-driven projects)
Inspection:	Everyone examines, trying to improve product, process and people
Integration test	Ensuring new functionality works immediately in existing system
Iterative process	A method to plan the entire project at only a high level at the start and plan portions to be done soon in detail, updating plans as more becomes known.
Journey maps	Simple visual showing how customers view experience
Just-in-time (JIT) planning	Describe work needed for current design at the last responsible moment

Kanban board	Visible information register that communicates work status as to do, in progress, or done
Lead time	Shorter lead time makes better service and faster feedback
Lean	Continuous delivery approach emphasizing eliminating waste of any kind
Lean (aka Kanban) lifecycle	Continuous workflow with highly visible information
Low-context culture	Straightforward, direct, and transparent communication in which what you say is what you mean and there are no hidden messages associated
Make process explicit	Ensure everyone understand how a process works
Manage flow	Teams focus on reducing time to complete work
Metaphor	Compare project vision to seemingly different thing in such a manner that key similarities are emphasized
Minimize WIP	Focus on the work that has been started and finish it promptly
Minimal marketable feature (MMF)	A single fully-functional, tested feature a customer could use
Minimum marketable release (MMR)	Fully functional product release with fewest acceptable features
Minimum viable product (MVP)	The simplest version of a product with just enough features to gain quick customer feedback
Money for nothing	Agreement to pay contractor portion if future work is terminated
Monochronic time (M-Time)	A focus on one thing at a time and it requires careful planning. Time is considered to be specific and real
MoSCoW	Prioritization technique of must, should, could, and will not have

Objective milestones	Decision points based on objective evaluation of progress toward working systems
Openness	Seek new ideas, ask for help when needed
Optimize the whole	Teams look at what the whole needs, not just their needs
Pair programming	Practice of one programmer writing while another reviews, two minds are better than one
Persona	Fictional username, description, and values for solution
Pivot	Changing direction on next sprint based upon customer desires
Plan at multiple levels	Project and release planning early and more detailed as needed
Plan-driven	(aka predictive, traditional, or waterfall) approach to projects where the entire project is planned in detail early in the project and great effort is expended to control any changes
Planning poker (games)	Method for team to quickly relatively size specific stories
Polychronic time (P-Time)	A focus on human interactions and relations over time and materialistic things. Work completion time is often unpredictable as it is done at one's own pace.
Portfolio vision	Description of desired future state of value streams and solutions
Practice servant leadership	A person in authority's primary role is to help others perform better
Premortem	Brainstorming description of what could go wrong
Prioritized backlog	Desired products prioritized by business value and risk
Product	The deliverables that are created in an agile project

Product backlog	A wish-list of things that may be created by the project team
Product backlog refining	A planning meeting to understand, slice, and estimate the time to create each user story to ensure each meets the definition of ready.
Product increment	The deliverables created and accepted during a sprint
Product owner	The person who represents the client or customer and other stakeholders, prioritizing work and making timely decisions, enabling an agile project team.
Product roadmap	Visual showing high-level plans of products expected to be created during each release
Product vision	Description of customer satisfaction and alignment with business objectives at an initially high level
Production-ready	Milestone early in transition when product is tested and complete, and users are capable to accept
Program	Large development effort involving multiple coordinated teams—also known as team of teams approach
Project Management Institute (PMI)	Large professional organization that supports all approaches to project management, including agile
Proven approach	Milestone early in construction when approach is verified to reduce risk
Queue duration and length	Time work spends waiting, lean attempts to reduce it
Refactoring	Simplifying and cleaning a product to make it stable and maintainable
Refine requirements	Use feedback to progressively understand true needs

Release	Period when functionality is created and transitioned to users
Release backlog	The work that is planned to be completed in current release
Release decision	Determination that product and support are ready for transition and customer is ready to successfully use product
Requirement	A condition or capability needed by a user to solve a problem or achieve an objective
Release planning	Scope current release and envision high-level view of future
Respect	Everyone gives and feels respect, everyone contributes, team strength is collaboration, give each other permission
Retrospective	ID lessons learned, plan to improve people, process, and product
Right-sized	Ensuring stories are small, understood, and testable
Risk-adjusted backlog	To-do prioritized list of work to both create product and reduce risk
Risk-based spike	Short time-boxed work to address specific risk
Savage summary	The briefest description of an idea or tool to help people understand it
Scaled Agile Framework (SAFe)	An enterprise-level framework that facilitates planning at various levels such as team, program, and portfolio
Scrum	Most used agile approach that emphasizes planning and managing
Scrum master	The person who facilitates and guides the team to improve performance, removing roadblocks, so the members can focus on their work
Scrum of scrums	Concept wherein each team is represented in a meeting of all teams

Servant leadership	Leader focuses on needs of the followers first through integrating followers needs with project goals, honesty, delegation, and empowerment.
Share knowledge	Deliberatively capture and share tacit knowledge
Shared vision	Quickly learn desires of key stakeholders and alignment with business objectives
Shift left	Perform as much testing and risk reduction early to gain feedback as soon as possible so needed changes can be started quickly
Simplicity	Do what is needed and no more, take small simple steps, use sheerest possible design to meet today's requirement
Slice a story	Break down an epic or large story into small enough portions that teams can estimate the effort needed to create them, and then commit to finishing them within a single sprint
Small releases	Provide tested, working product often to deploy to users
Solutions	Deliverables that are usable, desirable, and functional in helping customers achieve desired outcomes
Spikes	Short, time-boxed effort to test concept or reduce risk
Sponsor	The person who wants the project to be completed, provides resources, often controls the budget, represents top management, and makes major decisions
Sprint (aka increment)	Short period when committed to deliverables are created
Sprint backlog	The work that is committed to be completed in current sprint

Sprint daily scrum	A 15-minute meeting for each team member to share what they did yesterday, what they plan today, and what may get in the way
Sprint planning	A planning meeting to plan the work outputs and methods for the upcoming sprint
Sprint retrospective	Review meeting in which the team and scrum master reflect on what worked well and what did not and plan to improve.
Sprint review (aka demo)	A demonstration meeting when the team shows product created and PO determines if it meets definition of done
Stakeholder	Someone affected by the project such as an end-user, indirect user, or manager
Stakeholder vision	Milestone at end of inception with initial scope, technology, risk, and so on are agreed
Storyboard	A simple tool that uses sticky notes on a board to present tasks with their status (to do, in progress, or done), and sometimes relations among them (predecessor and successor relations) and/or other information
Story map	Visual with product features on top and supporting detail below
Story point	Estimate by team of complexity and size of specific work in story form
Subject-matter expert (SME)	Is an authority regarding a subject or discipline such as technology, process, business, or any other aspect that is of importance to the project.
Sufficient functionality	Milestone late in construction when the MMR is achieved, and cost is okay to release product

Support readiness	Sufficient instruction, service, and anything else needed to ensure customers can successfully use deliverables
Sustainable pace	Amount of work team can consistently produce well
Task card	Sticky note or index card showing work item name and other info
Task switching	Time and concentration are lost when changing the work a person is doing
Team member	A person who works on a project in cooperation with others to develop the solution for the stakeholder.
Test plan	Determine how you will verify work is acceptable before coding
Test-driven development	The practice of writing tests to be used before writing code
Testing	Evaluating to ensure that the deliverable meets requirements, and it also serves as an important feedback mechanism
3C process	Task card with conversations and confirmation of understanding
Throughput	The average number of units produced in a time duration
Timebox	A defined number of hours or days to complete an agreed upon amount of work
Transactional leadership	Leader with position authority sues rewards and punishment to gain compliance
Transformational leadership	Leader aims to develop trust and align personal values of individuals (followers) to accomplish vision and mission of the organization
Transition phase	Readiness determined and solution released into production with the support to help customer achieve desired outcomes

Transparency	All people openly present the facts as they are to create necessary trust
Trend analysis	Quantitative review of changes in performance over time
Tuckman's team stage development model	A gradual and sequential process of moving from forming to storming, norming, and finally, performing stage of team development
Unit test	Ensuring small function or classes work properly
User story	Need described by who wants it, how they will use it, and why
Value stream mapping	Visual flowchart identifying value and nonvalue activities
Variance analysis	Quantitative review of difference between expected and actual
Velocity	The forecasted number of story points a team can do in one sprint
Verification and validation	Ensuring quality at multiple levels and time periods
Waiting	Delays may mean later feedback and task switching, work is not ready
Work culture	Shared beliefs, values, and practices of individuals or groups in an organization, and it influences norms and behavior of both individuals and groups of that organization
WIP	Work that has been started, but has not yet been completed, costs worktime, is not yet of value, and may be obsolete
Work item pool	All work to do: new requirements, defects, training, and so on

About the Authors

Vittal S. Anantatmula is a Professor of project management at Western Carolina University, where he has served as the director of the masters in project management program. Vittal was a recipient of Endeavour Executive Fellow from the Government of Australia. He also received the university scholar award and excellence in teaching and research awards at Western Carolina University. Dr. Anantatmula is a global guest professor at Keio University, Yokohama, Japan since 2015. He is the director and board member of the Project Management Institute Global Accreditation Center (PMI-GAC) since 2016. He serves on the editorial board of several scholarly journals. In the past, he taught at the George Washington University, worked in the petroleum and power industries for several years as an electrical engineer and project manager, and as a consultant in several international organizations, including the World Bank. Dr. Anantatmula has authored more than 80 publications, eight books, nine book chapters, and about 60 conference papers. He received his PhD from the George Washington University, and he is a certified project management professional (PMP).

Timothy J. Kloppenborg is a Professor Emeritus from Xavier University. Tim has over 100 publications, including 12 books, mostly dealing with leadership and project management. Dr. Kloppenborg is the founding collection editor for Business Expert Press's portfolio and project management collection that contains over 50 books. Tim has worked in manufacturing, construction, and research, and is a retired U.S. Air Force Reserve officer. He has consulted, trained, and taught on six continents. He holds a BS in business from Benedictine College, an MBA from Western Illinois University, and a PhD in Operations Management from University of Cincinnati. He is a certified project management professional (PMP), an Agile Certified Practitioner (PMI-ACP), and a Disciplined Agile Senior Scrum Master (DASSM).

Index